The First-Time Trainer,

Second Edition

A Step-by-Step Quick Guide for Managers, Supervisors, and New Training Professionals

Tom W. Goad

AMACOM
American Management Association
New York • Atlanta • Brussels • Chicago • Mexico City • San Francisco
Shanghai • Tokyo • Toronto • Washington, D. C.

American Management Association
www.amanet.org

Special discounts on bulk quantities of AMACOM books are available to corporations, professional associations, and other organizations. For details, contact Special Sales Department, AMACOM, a division of American Management Association, 1601 Broadway, New York, NY 10019.
Tel: 800-250-5308   Fax: 518-891-2372
Email: specialsls@amanet.org
Website: www.amacombooks.org/go/specialsales
To view all AMACOM title go to: www.amacombooks.org

This publication is designed to provide accurate and authoritative information in regard to the subject matter covered. It is sold with the understanding that the publisher is not engaged in rendering legal, accounting, or other professional service. If legal advice or other expert assistance is required, the services of a competent professional person should be sought.

Library of Congress Cataloging-in-Publication Data

Goad, Tom W.
    The first-time trainer : a step-by-step quick guide for managers, supervisors, and new training professionals / Tom W. Goad. — 2nd ed.
        p. cm.
    Includes bibliographical references and index.
    ISBN-13: 978-0-8144-1559-7
    ISBN-10: 0-8144-1559-9
    1. Employees—Training of. 2. Training. I. Title.
    HF5549.5.T7G535 2010
    658.3'124—dc22

                                                              2009024840

Printing number

10   9   8   7   6   5   4   3   2   1

American Management Association
    www.amanet.org

Contents

American Management Association
www.amanet.org

List of Exhibits

American Management Association
www.amanet.org

About the Revised Edition

Some things change; some things stay the same. Training has done both over the years since *The First-Time Trainer* was published. Technology, particularly in the form of electronic learning—e-learning—has redesigned the landscape for training, as it has become a primary way training is designed, developed, delivered, and tracked. The Internet, with all its connectivity, is literally a worldwide classroom, open for business around the clock. Yet, classroom training is alive and thriving and even increases when the economy sours. Today, the trainer has more choices than ever to facilitate learning. Successful organizations depend on this to keep them viable, demanding that the trainer be competent in this expanded spectrum of training, taking in both old and new choices.

A second new development challenges the trainer more today than in the past. The nature of the workplace and the employees who are learners continues to change. Diversity in the traditional sense is just that: highly diverse, with globalization changing and enriching the cultural mix. The multigenerational workforce is more pronounced, with sharp contrasts between older and younger workers. This is noticeably true when multigenerational learners sit side by side in a classroom or participate in an online training session.

This revised edition of *The First-Time Trainer* gives these two significant developments their proper treatment in the trainer's tool kit.

The basic principles of training—the eight steps to training—are as solid as ever. This revised edition brings the book up-to-date with the times, ready to serve you as you launch, or perhaps continue, you career as a facilitator of learning. Terminology changes: for instance, the trainer may be referred to as a workplace

American Management Association
www.amanet.org

learning professional. And you'll hear terms like wikis, blogs, rapid e-learning, podcasts, Webcasts, and asynchronous training, to name a few. New terms come along, but the task is the same: increasing the skills and knowledge of learners so they and their organizations perform most effectively. Training is still the best way to make certain employees as learners perform at their best. Training contributes directly and positively to the bottom line for all organizations. *The First-Time Trainer, Second Edition*, is dedicated to this concept— and to the people who make it happen.

Like the original, *The First-Time Trainer, Second Edition*, provides you with a solid basis for becoming a trainer, without any extra material getting in the way. The revised edition has added background material in selected areas so that you can delve deeper into the details of training. A new appendix provides you with more in-depth information in the form of guidelines. They cover the following:

1. Guidelines for how people learn—we're continually discovering more about this as we learn more about how the brain functions.
2. Guidelines for professional development—as all professional people know, there can never be too much of this.
3. Guidelines for dealing with multiple generations in the workplace—as the workplace continues to broaden in the cultural and age diversity of the people who work, meaning trainers must be aware of these differences.
4. Guidelines for conducting evaluation, including additional tools—always a challenge, and always needed.
5. Guidelines for determining whether or not the training is worth the expense—return on investment (ROI)—the literal and figurative bottom line of all training.

The Eight Steps to Effective Training are, together, the first step toward making you an effective trainer. With this new appendix, you have the material you'll need to take additional steps toward becoming a more professional and fully versed trainer. You may also want to refer to them as you cover the basic training steps in the main text.

A Word for the First-Time Trainer

Managers face challenges every day. One of the biggest is keeping employee skills updated. When skills are rendered obsolete by each new technological breakthrough—or the competition beats you to the punch—the challenge is greatly magnified. This is true for both the profit and the nonprofit sectors, large and small. The task of training employees is something facing more and more managers, professional people, and others in the workplace. Developing employee talent keeps the best organizations on the leading edge. It's often the only way to achieve desired results. Yet, with tight budgets and flattened organizations, and especially in small organizations with scarce resources, training is more easily talked about than done. So how do you get people trained? The easiest way is to turn them over to a competent, well-funded training department. But, often, in the many organizations that do not have this option, training falls into the lap of managers or relatively inexperienced professional trainers.

When that happens, you have a critical job to do and perhaps little experience to call upon. Therefore, this book will serve as your guide. Every effort has been made to provide just the right amount of information and guidance—clearly and concisely, with no extra frills—to turn you into an effective trainer.

We all want to do our best, regardless of what the job is. Accordingly, this book represents best practice. It describes a process that has been boiled down to precisely what a manager or new trainer needs to know to get the job done: the eight steps to effective training.

Not every training session you may be called upon to deliver will require that all eight steps be carried out to their fullest; your

American Management Association
www.amanet.org

task is relatively simple and straightforward for a short training presentation, for example. At the other extreme, some training can take months and large numbers of qualified persons to develop. Consider, for example, the training that must accompany a new multimillion-dollar weapons system or the installation of a new management information system in a company. The eight steps are summarized in this introduction and explained more fully at the end of Step One.

Numerous exhibits throughout the book facilitate your use of the material presented. Many of them summarize ideas explained in detail in the text; you may find it helpful to scan the exhibits to get a quick overview of the book or to refresh your memory later.

Eight Steps to Effective Training.

Step One	**Facilitate learning**—This element is the key to trainer success and includes how to implement the other seven steps.
Step Two	**Focus on performance**—Establish the objective of the training, and make sure you're on track—*before* you start.
Step Three	**Focus on learning**—Make sure the training provides the maximum possibility for participant learning, with emphasis on how adults and organizations learn.
Step Four	**Be prepared**—Develop the materials you'll need, bringing them together in the most effective order and making sure everything is ready to go.
Step Five	**Deliver effectively**—Learn the communication skills you'll need to present your training session successfully.
Step Six	**Get learners involved**—Learn how to develop the best in all participants and different ways to deliver the training.
Step Seven	**Get feedback**—Develop ways to determine training success.
Step Eight	**Improve continuously**—Keep your trainer's portfolio up-to-date and strengthen your skills as a trainer.

Training is best approached as a system, so you'll notice some overlap between steps. For example, questioning techniques are applicable to both getting people involved (Step Six) and evaluation (Step Seven). You'll find cross-references to provide integration of the steps. A summary at the beginning of each step will help you quickly determine where you are, what is useful, and where to go next. You can come back and read the rest of the book another time, and you're encouraged to do so. Another approach you might take is to scan Steps One through Eight to get an idea of what functions and tools are available and then use the eight steps as needed. Either way, read, enjoy, and prosper! And, remember, common sense and good management skills will take you a long way as a trainer.

American Management Association
www.amanet.org

Introduction

"Training now enables a country's labor force to attain world-class productivity while still paying an emerging country's wages for at least eight or ten years."
— Peter Drucker, *The Changing World Economy*, 2002

Training has grown into one of the most critical requirements for success in a highly competitive global marketplace. The reasons are clear. Increased emphasis on human resources effectiveness, including such concepts as talent management, human capital, and human resources as an investment, is one. Worker skills must be continually updated. Diversity, workplace laws, shortages of skilled workers, persistent functional illiteracy, and intensive competition continue to influence, and often redefine, the way people work. Add the fact that technology alone causes constant workplace change, and the spotlight falls brighter than ever on the trainer. As more and more managers, team leaders, professionals, and others are finding out, there comes a time when we must all function as trainers. Customers demand it, competition forces it, and employees need it to survive. Simply put, there's greater need for training.

Sometimes there's no formal training department, or the workload is too great even if there is one, or the requirement is so technical that the training department has no one who is qualified. The result is that many people are called upon to train. This may include people who have never trained before as well as professional trainers who find their workload and level of competence stretched by the increased demand and highly technical subject matter.

American Management Association
www.amanet.org

The Purpose of This Book

Since you may be new to training or have had little opportunity to train, you'll appreciate the singular purpose of this book: to serve as a clearly stated set of proven guidelines to use when you conduct training. These are the functions you'll perform—no more or no less—to be a successful trainer. They're the same whether they're used for a once-in-a-lifetime performance or become something you'll need for the rest of your career. (It's more likely to be the latter, the way training continues to prove critical to the organizations it serves.) The session you're called on to do may range across a wide spectrum of training, including:

- Giving your boss a fifteen-minute overview and demonstration of a work project
- Offering a one-week training program that will allow your company to provide faster customer service
- Preparing a two-hour podcast session on implementing a new method of conducting performance appraisals
- Conducting a long-term program of converting your company from a traditional divisional organization with multiple layers to a matrix organization that emphasizes a team approach to projects
- Developing an online course for new supervisors to improve their verbal communication skills
- Appearing briefly on the agenda of a planning committee to explain how you're preparing to comply with new labor legislation
- Conducting a three-day workshop designed to bring in two hundred people who have never worked together to form a team to implement a new government contract

These represent but a few of the possible combinations. A common situation for some managers is that they must deal with all the above. Whatever the nature of the training, from brief presentations to full-blown, formal training courses, the principles are the same. It's these success-driven principles that are laid down in this book in the form of eight steps—the eight steps to effective training. An important fact to bear in mind: They apply across the board, for all types of training using all forms of delivery, and in all types of organizations.

About Training

Let's look at the purpose of training in today's organizations—both for- and not-for-profit—and why training continues to be so important.

The Purpose of Training

Training exists to facilitate the process of making organizations, and the people within them, more effective. For organizations to thrive, the function of training must be implemented to its fullest. Employee talent must be developed—and enhanced—to the greatest extent possible. Training must move and flow. It works best when it becomes an integral part of the organizational process, from strategic planning (e.g., including training as a fundamental part of ongoing organizational development) to reviewing the profit and loss statement (e.g., measuring training's effectiveness). Take the example mentioned earlier of giving your boss a fifteen-minute overview and demonstration of a work project. Suppose the marketing team needs the input in order to start promoting the product, thus making the session, even if only a fifteen-minute one, of the utmost importance. (And sometimes you're lucky to get that much time, making it all the more critical to do a good job.)

Why Training Is So Important

Information and knowledge drive most businesses, and often training is the only way the information and knowledge, and attendant skills, can be provided. It has become clearer than ever that those organizations that are succeeding in today's marketplace are the ones that help their employees perform to their fullest potential.

Tributes to the importance of training abound in the business news. Studies of successful organizations emphasize this fact by regularly showing how training has been key to companies' making it to the top in their industries. Training's reason for being is to make people more effective and therefore more valuable. The more knowledge and skills employees have, the more effective the company is. And this holds true for nonprofits, too. The relationship is direct and clear. Check your own information sources and the latest business news, and you'll realize that successful organizations most likely view training as an important part of the success equation. Some of the more important reasons for that include:

- *Technology That Continues to Virtually Upgrade Itself.* The people who implement technology must upgrade their skills to keep up with it. This is one of the greatest challenges facing everyone today, from the top to the bottom of organizations.
- *Organizations That Have Become So-Called Learning Organizations.* That means that the people in them must use training as one method of continuing the learning process, a process greatly facilitated by online, or electronic, learning. Things move so fast that we must constantly be on the alert to learn how to keep up and, for the few, to stay ahead.
- *Team Orientation.* Members of the work group must be cross-trained to perform one another's jobs. Teams remain as strong as ever as a workplace approach to success.
- *Fewer Workers to Pass Things Down to Because of Massive Downsizing.* Unfortunately, the work itself doesn't get downsized, just the number of people available to do it, which places a further workplace load on the survivors. Downsizing turmoil continues as the process keeps rolling along.
- *Workplaces That Continue to Become yet More Complex.* This isn't so true in fast-growing job areas like fast food and service industries, but it is definitely so in professions that offer the best rewards. All indications are that this situation will continue.
- *Government Intervention in the Workplace.* This is particularly true with respect to far-reaching laws that have an impact on work and workers. It applies from the federal level down through the local community. Occasionally a law specifies that training be conducted.
- *Functional Illiteracy and the Need to Train People in Job Basics, Particularly Entry-Level Ones.* Estimates are that one in five adults in the United States is functionally illiterate; these people lack basic reading, writing, speaking, computing, or decision-making skills.
- *Multicultural Workplaces, Where Workers May Speak Many Languages Other Than English as Their First Language.* This is an ongoing result of globalization, making it imperative that people who work together be able to communicate well.

- *Multigenerational Workplaces, Where Workers Are Far Apart Not Only in Age but in Their Grasp of the Latest Technology.* People simply don't retire; older workers must learn to use new technology, and there may be differences in how they learn as well as in their motivation to do so.

Many of these represent areas where you may be called upon as a trainer.

The training process can be highly formalized and long term or quite informal and brief. The key is that learners come out of the process with new or stronger skills. Whereas the purpose of developing an organization is to make it more effective, the act of developing its people and their talents through training is to make individuals more effective in achieving organization goals.

A Word About E-Learning and Technology

Electronic learning—e-learning—comprises computer-based training (e.g., training via a CD and a personal computer) and training delivered via the Internet. The Internet is a workplace where learners are digitally connected and can learn continually. It simply means that each time a worker sits down at a work station, a training session can be initiated without waiting for a course to be convened, a classroom readied, and an instructor brought in. Everything else about the eight steps of training stays the same—it's just that training can be offered quickly and effectively. This is discussed in more detail as appropriate throughout the eight steps, particularly in Step Four, Be Prepared.

Use of the Internet brings other useful tools for training, such as blogs (online journals), wikis (Web sites that can be accessed and changed by users), social networking Web sites, and multiple ways of communicating. Training continues to benefit from software developments in the form of applications and training management tools. These have the capacity to improve the training process—provided the trainer uses the tools to their best advantage.

An overall advantage of technology, and particularly e-learning, is that it provides multiple ways of delivering training, a boon for people who have different learning styles. It also allows training to be disseminated rapidly, which you may find referred to as rapid e-learning.

A Word About Today's Diverse and Multigenerational Workforce

Today's workforce is the most diversified it has ever been. Think of a virtual corporation, where employees located in all corners of the world are working for the same corporation, interacting as if they were in the same room. Languages are different, ages are different—more and more workers are putting off retirement (for a variety of reasons) and staying at work or are re-entering the workplace. Older workers may well be novices at electronic devices, whereas the younger worker sitting at the next desk literally grew up with them (we're all familiar with the story about the adult asking a grandchild for help in using an electronic gadget). All this, combined with the more traditional forms of diversity, must be factored into the broad picture of the people being trained. It can make a difference between success and failure.

Now let's find out more about the first step toward effective training facilitation.

American Management Association
www.amanet.org

Step One

Facilitate Learning

"Learning and development professionals have got to think like line executives who constantly deal with customers and suppliers, both internal and external."

—Stephen Covey, *Training*, February 2006

The successful trainer facilitates learning. It's as simple as that. Facilitating means assisting adults in acquiring the skills and knowledge required by the workplace. These skills and knowledge may range from work rules a new employee needs to know, to how to operate a computer-aided design software system for an engineer, to how a manager can motivate employees (possibly spread around the globe) to increase production in the wake of massive layoffs. One of the key growth areas for training has been such softer issues as maintaining motivation, fostering interpersonal communication, nurturing self-esteem, achieving maximum potential, preventing sexual harassment, managing stress, and promoting healthier lifestyles. Clearly there is no limit on the topics that may need to be covered at some time or another. And, with the use of social Web sites on the Internet and technology that delivers training anytime, anywhere, training has expanded well beyond the workplace. Principles and techniques explained in this book work for all training needs and applications. See Exhibit 1-1 for a representative list of major training applications.

American Management Association
www.amanet.org

Exhibit 1-1. Major application categories of training.

- *Executive development.* Includes leadership training, advanced executive degree programs, mentoring programs, rotations through various divisions of the organization, special assignments; deals with highest-level management leadership skills such as managing change and strategic decision making; aimed at corporate-level management.

- *Management development.* Includes strategic planning skills, leadership, networking with other managers, degree programs, management of change, time management, project management, coaching, goal setting, and mentoring.

- *Supervisory development.* Includes basic interpersonal communication skills, how to make decisions, how to give orders, coaching employees, setting objectives, time management, and other basic skills that newly promoted supervisors might need.

- *Professional development.* Covers a wide variety of training, such as interpersonal communication skills, stress management, computer literacy, and specific discipline-related skills (e.g., finance, purchasing, engineering, scientific, health care); a broad area of training covering basic, advanced, and refresher training.

- *Technical skills.* Continues as one of the largest growth areas because of ever-evolving technology. Training associated with getting work accomplished; includes computer skills, manufacturing processes, using particular systems and equipment, carrying out policies and procedures, and flight training; some overlap with professional development.

- *Literacy skills.* Includes the fundamental skills needed to be able to read, write, speak, compute, and make decisions in entry-level jobs within an organization; process of making employees functionally literate, as well as training those already literate to move to higher levels.

- *Marketing and sales.* This ranges from training new sales representatives, to providing information on new products, to planning and research skills for marketing managers; involves the motivational aspects of marketing and interpersonal communication skills required.

- *Safety, health, and workplace laws.* This is designed to ensure a safe, healthy workplace while reducing costs related to maintaining safety health and dealing with legal issues; increasingly includes aspects of job stress and wellness training for a healthier lifestyle; includes drug and substance abuse training and training in legal areas related to the workplace such as sexual harassment prevention and other requirements that must be complied with.

- *Orientation.* This is for new employees to ensure they get off to a good start; formality varies from a few minutes to several weeks; ranges from basics about the workplace such as where the cafeteria is located to a detailed indoctrination on the company's culture.
- *Organization development.* This includes training conducted in relation to interventions to manage organization change, such as quality assurance programs, Six Sigma, customer service, and team building.

Training is a facilitation of learning. It focuses on identifying, ensuring, and helping to develop, through a carefully planned process, the key competencies that enable individuals to perform their jobs more efficiently. Although our concern here is workplace learning, the concept extends to training in such areas as learning how to plant an organic garden or to throw a clay pot; how to do your own plumbing or plan your vacation; or how to be a Scout leader.

You might think that a trainer is a person who may fill a number of roles, but the number-one role is to facilitate learning. When you've completed a training session, you should expect that participants will have gained knowledge or acquired skills they didn't previously have. Think of it as the process of filling a gap—the difference between what participants know or can do and what they need to know or do—called *gap analysis* (see Step Two). The best way to ensure that this happens is to consider yourself the facilitator of the process. Sometimes, particularly if their jobs depend on it, participants will learn even if the process is improperly or ineffectively done (more on this in Step Three). If you think back to the teachers and trainers you've had, you'll likely agree that the best ones were those who allowed learning to take place, as opposed to those who considered themselves the experts and didn't let you forget it (and sometimes got in the way).

A further word about gaps: It could well be that the gap between diverse and multigenerational learners is your greatest challenge. The solution, as will be noted throughout the eight steps, is variety in how training is designed, developed, and delivered.

Step One Summary

This step, facilitation, provides the background needed to acquire skills. Since the primary role of a trainer is to facilitate learning, it is essential that every trainer approach any project from the perspective of helping learning to happen rather than attempting to force it. Key materials are:

- A detailed definition of training
- Skills trainers need for success
- Diversity and multigenerational learners
- Continuous learning concept
- Skills related to knowledge learning and technology that are essential to today's workplace, providing the knowledge framework to successfully facilitate training
- Overview of the remaining seven steps and how to apply them

Skills Trainers Need—Overview

To be effective facilitators of learning, trainers must have a number of skills. They include but certainly are not limited to:

- *Managerial Ability.* The entire training process requires effective management to ensure success, especially within tight budgets. A trainer manages time (including the time learners are away from their jobs for training), resources, and funds, as well as staff members.
- *Communications Skills.* A complete repertoire of these skills includes the ability to motivate and familiarity with electronic methods.
- *Analytical and Problem-Solving Skills.* Analysis is an ongoing requirement.
- *Information Literacy.* Workers need to find information and implement solutions to problems.
- *Computer Literacy.* Because so much information is digitized, communications rely on automation and digital technology, and computers deliver a significant amount of training conducted.

Take a brief personal inventory of your own skills, and you'll likely see you're already in good shape for your new training role.

The Impact of Diversity and Multigenerational Learners

Diversity is one of the words most commonly used to describe today's workplace, and for good reason. Many companies are discovering that if they make the most of diversity and manage it to a purposeful end, productivity and effectiveness go up. It's a good return on investment. Because of globalization, management may have no choice but to make the most of a vastly diverse workforce. Diversity continues to suggest more than divergent cultural and racial backgrounds. It has grown to encompass as well:

- People with disabilities
- People who speak different languages
- Women, who are continuing to enter and move up in the workplace in large numbers
- Disadvantaged people
- Older people
- People who are functionally illiterate
- People of various sexual orientations
- People with various religious beliefs

There's another aspect of diversity that needs to be included— one dealing with workplace age differences. There are actually four generations in today's workplace: persons born before or during World War II; baby boomers, who were born after the war (between 1946 and 1964); Generation X, who were born between 1965 and 1980; and Generation Y (also called millennials and the Net Generation), who were born in the 1980s and 1990s. Having workers from three different generations (and possibly all four generations, as noted) is increasingly common today, and the difference between the technology orientation of the youngest (say a seventeen-year-old) and the oldest (say a sixty-five-year-old) is tremendous. How the two learn, what they are capable of doing, and particularly how they adapt to different training delivery methods varies considerably. Accordingly, your training approach needs to accommodate everyone. This is one of the exciting challenges of training, and there's plenty you can do to help deal with diversity. (This aspect of your training challenge is addressed in Step Five.)

Continuous Learning

Continuous learning is at the heart of the learning organization (see Step Three) and thus must be foremost in the mind of all managers and trainers. Like organizations, people must continually learn if they are to be successful and remain competitive. Technology, which seems to move at the speed of light, is a primary driver of the need to keep learning. Competition plays a key role, as well.

The explosion of information keeps us well supplied with material to learn from. What this means is that the trainer and the manager need to create an environment of continuous learning. Formal training sessions are necessary. So are opportunities to learn and grow, such as opportunities for taking classes outside work or learning by watching others or having access to an information base that people can use to learn on their own. Purchasing built-in training with new software packages and communications systems is another example of how to ensure continuous learning. This is where the creative trainer can greatly enhance learning on the part of all people on the job.

Electronic learning—e-learning—makes opportunities to learn a twenty-four-hour-a-day, seven-days-a-week proposition. With device portability, learning can occur just about anywhere a person might be. This is one of the developments of training that has brought new energy to the training process—but not without a cost in development, as well as stress on learners.

Trainer Skills

The skills needed for the future workplace are quite different from, and probably more complex than, the ones that got us to this point in our organizational lives. These new skills are some of the most important ones trainers are involved with. Indeed, there are skills we'll need down the road that haven't even been identified yet! A key question emerges: "If we must continually learn, what skills must we acquire?" Fortunately, there's plenty of guidance here. These key skills are shown in Exhibit 1-2. It's not a long list, but each element is vital. It's no coincidence that these are skills you need for virtually any job today.

Exhibit 1-2. Key workplace skills.

- *Information Literacy.* The ability to find, access, evaluate, and use information—possibly the most important skill in today's knowledge-driven workplace.
- *Interpersonal Communication Skills.* Includes all aspects of how people communicate. This is often called "good people skills" and applies at all levels, particularly the management level.
- *Problem Solving and Decision Making.* Skills increasingly required of people at all levels of organizations.
- *Creativity and Innovation.* The ability to generate fresh ideas and new ways of doing things.
- *Computer Literacy.* The ability to use the power of computers, including software applications, communication techniques, and the Internet.

Information Literacy

Much has already been said about the knowledge- or information-driven economy, which in turns means a knowledge-driven workplace. Just about everything we do involves acquiring and applying information in a knowledgeable way. First we have data, which the Internet, via the computer, has given us in enormous quantities (often too great). Next we turn the data into information or glean from them potentially useful information. From the information, we gain knowledge that allows us to be competitive and to succeed on the job. This is where training comes in. From knowledge comes (we hope) the wisdom that sustains us, propelling us to succeed. Keep this thought in mind when developing and implementing training. For short-term operations, it may not mean much. But, for the long haul, it can help keep us on track to develop meaningful long-term training and development for all workers—full-time employees, contract workers, part-timers, and all the others.

Information literacy has been defined as the ability to access, evaluate, and use information from a variety of sources. It sounds simple—but think for a moment about each segment of this sentence. To access information means that you know how to get your hands on potentially relevant information, which in turn means you must know where to find it. Evaluating the mountains of information showered upon us can be an enormous task in itself. To use the information once it is selected is the mark of the truly successful manager and trainer. An information-literate person has the following characteristics:

- Recognizes the *need* for information before taking action.
- Recognizes that *accurate and complete* information is essential in order to make intelligent decisions.
- Formulates *questions*, based on information needs, that will lead to desired information.
- Develops successful, possibly diverse, *search strategies*, based on all potential sources.
- Accesses information *sources*—digitally based (e.g., Internet, World Wide Web, individuals, data banks), analog, human, and other sources.
- *Evaluates* information to discern its relevance, setting aside anything that is irrelevant (which might easily be the bulk of it).
- *Organizes* information for practical application.
- *Integrates* new information into the existing body of knowledge (so that it fits in and potentially enhances it).
- *Applies* the information to critical thinking and problem solving (not hesitating to reenter the process at any step when the need arises).

And one last point: If you don't know how to apply the information once you've acquired it, you're not fully information literate.

Interpersonal Communication Skills

This skill set, which includes the full spectrum of how humans communicate with each other, has always been vital to workplace success, but, if anything, it is more important today because of such practices as empowerment and working at home, along with the multitude of ways we communicate. The skills include:

- *Having the ability to read and comprehend*, sometimes as a rapid response to a particular work situation.
- *Having the ability to write.* This encompasses memos, e-mail messages that are well thought out yet quickly written, letters, reports, documents, and all those other communications, written and digital (e.g., e-mail, blogs, text messaging, Twittering), that

are common in the workplace. (This includes training materials, discussed in Step Four, and particularly material written for on-line learning.)

- *Speaking* (addressed in depth in Step Five).
- *Listening.* This is an absolute necessity in the age of empower-ment, team orientation, coaching, and mentoring.
- *Using nonverbal skills.* This means the ability to sense how you are perceived as a total person (e.g., from your body language as well as from your words) when communicating and the ability to per-ceive someone else's total person and to fully comprehend what that person has to say.
- *Coaching and mentoring.* These involve the total spectrum of communication skills, as both require working closely with the learner. Rapport must be built up between you and the person you are coaching or mentoring. (See Step Four for more on these skills.)

There is a direct relationship between success and having good "people" skills. Yet another consideration, one we're still learning to deal with adequately, is how to accommodate the fact that many of the people we communicate with speak English as a second lan-guage, if at all. This is one of the challenges of a workplace that is diverse and multigenerational.

Problem Solving and Decision Making

One consequence of flattening in organizations is that more people than ever need good problem-solving and decision-making skills. The process is continually being pushed down to the lowest lev-els of the organization. If people are to become empowered in the workplace, they must have appropriate skills—that is, the ability to solve problems and make decisions. Managers want to hear solu-tions, not requests for advice on how to solve problems. Although it's a responsibility of managers to help develop others, the business environment today doesn't allow much time to pay a lot of attention to others.

Successful problem solvers have a proven problem-solving technique or model that they have mastered for solving challenges; many of these techniques contain most of the ones listed in Exhibit

1-3 (maybe all of them). The similarity of these actions to the eight steps to effective training isn't a coincidence.

Exhibit 1-3. A problem-solving model.

1. *Analysis.* Assess the problem to determine its causes (see Step Two for a detailed discussion of analysis).
2. *Solutions.* Identify alternatives to solve the problem.
3. *Selection.* Select one of the alternatives after weighing how well it will solve the problem (prioritize and know there is no perfect solution).
4. *Action.* Implement the selected solution (which may require the ability to overcome procrastination).
5. *Evaluation.* Assess how well the solution is working, and do not hesitate to make any needed corrections.

Creativity and Innovation

Successful companies have the ability to motivate employees to be creative and innovative. Encouraging risk taking and fostering an environment where failure is okay are fundamental elements of creative organizations. A number of approaches have successfully been taken here, and new techniques, including mind mapping (placing the main topic in the center and branching off in different directions with sub-topics), various thinking styles (thinking, using different, unconventional patterns), and special courses designed to take advantage of brain theories and strategies (e.g., left brain, right brain) have been developed. With carefully planned and executed training, people can learn on the job how to expand their creative horizons.

High-technology companies need creative employees if they are to stay on the cutting edge of competition—and so do all other organizations if they are to survive in the marketplace. Sometimes it is the person who can be creative in determining how to reduce the time that inventory stays on the shelf, for example, or figuring out how to take care of customer questions faster who can make the difference in the organization's success.

Computer Literacy

Computer literacy is more than knowing how to boot up a computer and generate a document with a word processor application package. For instance, it includes knowing at least the rudiments of an operating system such as Macintosh or Windows, or perhaps several systems. Some people find they must move between systems for a variety of reasons. Computer literacy assumes proficiency (even if one is a two-fingered typist) in word processing and means knowing the principles involved so that it isn't difficult to switch to a different word processor when the need arises. It could also mean knowing other applications such as spreadsheets, database management packages, and the company's customized software. (Games aren't on the list, although some people believe they should be—games are sometimes used in training.)

With the advent of such extensive use of e-learning, trainers must ultimately be able to effectively use learning systems that have become quite sophisticated. This includes programs that register learners, deliver and evaluate the training, and keep track of training that has been conducted. It also includes programs that convert existing materials such as digital presentations into a training format. Together, these are skills that more experienced trainers will have, although if you are experienced in advanced software packages, you will find it much easier to learn training program skills.

Proficiency in electronic messages such as e-mail and text messaging, from local to worldwide applications, comes in here. Computer literacy has expanded to include the ability to use the Internet and intranets (exclusive organizational networks), as the world in general and companies in particular become more digital. This is where the concept of computer literacy takes on a broader dimension: that of being truly digital (and we are reminded that electronic learning is totally digital). Communication skills have reached into the digital world and all it brings with it, including telecommunications.

The Eight Steps

This book is built around eight simple, interrelated steps. Your particular need could be simply to prepare or deliver training, and nothing more. However, most training requires that some degree of attention be paid to all eight steps.

Step One: Facilitate Learning

Step One largely entails being able to integrate adult learning principles into training from start to finish. It means recognizing that people learn best if given the room to do so and when they are properly motivated. Training used to refer to an instructor standing before a captive audience while delivering the word according to the experts and expecting the audience to absorb every word. That has become a thing of the past. Step One also includes adeptness at implementing the other seven steps. When the training exists on and is delivered by computer and over the Internet, it must still be motivational and completely relevant to what the learner needs to learn.

Step Two: Focus on Performance

Establishing training objectives and making sure you're on track *before starting* is essential for effective training. Front-end analysis—anything from looking at dwindling sales receipts to full-scale analysis of major organization functions—must be conducted before you can develop objectives for the training. Needs assessment helps identify performance deficiencies or perhaps areas where performance is adequate but improvement is desired. The identified needs are used to develop precise, measurable objectives, which drive training.

The first two steps make the remainder of the process much easier when they are done well. They also provide a road map for success.

Step Three: Focus on Learning

This step serves the purpose of making sure that training maximizes participant learning. It emphasizes how adults and organizations learn. Two key concepts—core competency and mastery of the organization and its employees—set successful organizations apart, and the most successful of these have people who have mastered the core skills the organization needs to succeed. Both concepts must be factored into any training. In addition, we need to focus on new ideas in learning and performance: the concept of the learning organization, learning how to learn, and new ways people learn and function, including multimodality (playing to all the senses and using as many ways to present the materials as possible, a concept you'll read more about it Step Three). You'll come across the term "talent": Trainers are expected to enhance and effectively manage the talents of learners.

Step Four: Be Prepared

If you were ever a Scout, you know exactly what this means. It's what the Olympian does for months, possibly years, before the event. It's what the chief executive of a corporation does before standing in front of a room full of financial analysts to report the company's latest developments and changes for the future. It's also what trainers must do if training is to be highly successful. It involves developing the materials, bringing them together in the most effective order, and making sure everything is ready to go. This ranges from such simple things as making sure there's an electrical outlet for a projector, to creating a four-day workshop for two thousand people tuned in via satellite from around the world—or glued to their work station terminals taking the training online.

Step Five: Deliver Effectively

This is where communication skills used to present a training session come into play and where learning principles and knowledge of training technology are manifested. If online learning is involved, the presenter's writing skills will be fully challenged. This step also requires accommodating diversity, and the broad range of beliefs, ages, experiences, and abilities of the learners add to the trainer's challenge. Group behavior in the classroom (and even in online sessions where learners can text message one another) is important to the trainer, as well. How a group performs and interacts during training can make a difference in how successful the outcome is. Finally, the trainer must know how to deal with individual behavior, particularly when behavioral challenges arise in a classroom situation.

Step Six: Get Learners Involved

One of the keys to adult learning is to get the participants involved on their own terms, whether they are in a classroom or online. This includes knowing how to bring out the best in them, as well as how to use different ways to deliver training. Unless you have a background in group behavior and exposure to the specifics of how to do this successfully, you'll have to acquire the necessary skills. Fortunately, there are plenty of ways to get people intimately involved in learning. This is where the concept of multimodality can help you improve training.

Step Seven: Get Feedback

Only through feedback can we determine if the desired new performance has been achieved through training. This step works best when feedback is sought and applied throughout the process, not just when training is over. Feedback during the design and development phases contributes to a better end product. Getting feedback requires more than giving tests. There are many ways to determine training success; for starters, refer to the carefully developed objectives identified in Step Two.

Step Eight: Improve Continuously

Continuous learning applies to everyone in today's workforce, including trainers. In some ways, it applies particularly to trainers because of the need for training to be relevant and up-to-date on the latest information on how people learn and perform on the job (as well as to keep up with technology). This is the process of keeping your trainer's portfolio up-to-date and strengthening your skills as a trainer.

   These are the eight steps that successful trainers have used to ply their trade for more than half a century, when training came into its own as a profession. (Actually, our ancestors used the same principles long before the work *training* came into being.) The key consideration is that they are proven steps; they will get the job done.

Using the Eight Steps for Various Situations

The examples shown in Exhibit 1-4 are based on two different possibilities—one from each end of the possible spectrum of requirements you may face. Extrapolate for situations that fall in between. The time available and the size of your budget will have a lot to say about how extensive each step along the way must be.

Exhibit 1-4. How to apply the eight steps to training situations.

	Short Presentation	*Major Training Event*
Step One: Facilitate learning.	Brief review of eight steps to refresh the concept of facilitator and review the steps you'll be using.	Review the eight steps to lock in the concept of facilitator and ensure that you deal thoroughly with all eight.
Step Two: Focus on performance.	Take time to identify the objective of the session; to provide specific information to a well-defined audience.	This is an important step; training for an extended length of time, covering highly technical subject matter, or addressing a large number of participants indicates a high level of need. There's a direct relationship between the length of the session and having multiple learning objectives, so it is critical to have objectives to keep you on track. Putting in the preparation time at the front end will save time overall.
Step Three: Focus on learning.	Give some thought to ways you can get participants to relate the presentation to their own experiences.	Building adult and other learning theory into the training will contribute to ultimate success. Use the sixteen learning principles (see Exhibit 3-1) as

(continues)

Exhibit 1-4. (*continued*)

	Short Presentation	*Major Training Event*
		a final checklist when the training is ready to be delivered. Think always of involvement and variety.
Step Four: Be prepared.	In a way, this is more important for a short session because there is no extra time to fall back and regroup. Never underestimate the need to be overprepared. Every second must be accounted for.	The nature of a longer session will dictate that you pay much attention to this step. Keep in mind the idea that variety will likely contribute positively to your training. You may find yourself using most, if not all, of the tools provided in this step. As a checklist, identify everything you think you may need before you begin.
Step Five: Deliver effectively.	This step is equally important regardless of the length of training. For shorter sessions, look through the guidelines in the step to determine which ones best fit your needs and the needs of your participants.	In a longer session, you will use more of the techniques. Of particular interest might be the use of a variety of methods while addressing the concept of multimodality. Here you'll have more opportunity to appeal to all learning styles. The length dictates that it be delivered effectively all the way through.
Step Six: Get learners involved.	There may be little chance to get participants involved in the session, although it's worth spending a little time to make sure that if there is a	Fully exploit this step, because doing so will affect the end result positively. In fact, the more time you spend with participants, the more vital it is that they become involved. Just think how

	Short Presentation	Major Training Event
	way, you use it. You can certainly get them mentally involved with a little forethought.	long you can sit still and listen to someone speak, no matter how fascinating the person is. Completion of previous steps will pay dividends here.
Step Seven: Get feedback.	You want to get at least a word or two from participants on how things went. It may be possible to hand out a feedback form, but only if relevant. Certainly you can do a self-check.	It's essential to evaluate the training. Do self-assessment, and be sure to get feedback from participants and their managers. Only through feedback can you make improvements to training. Build evaluation into the training.
Step Eight: Improve continuously.	If this is the only training you'll ever conduct, you can ignore this step. However, if there's a chance you may do it again, try to improve the presentation or other pertinent skills.	Here is where you must practice what you preach to participants: to continually improve. There are plenty of ways, so pay attention to the advice and direction in this step. Continued professional development will be obvious to participants and contribute to your continued success as a trainer.

You'll soon find that each step includes one or more tools designed to help you quickly and professionally prepare and deliver training. But don't hesitate to use your own ideas; being creative and spontaneous can push good training over the top to become great training.

Step Two

Focus on Performance

"A well-organized training session, based on clearly defined learning objectives, will give you the results you are striving for just about every time."

—Tom Goad, *Delivering Effective Training*, 1982

Effective training starts by clearly identifying the organization's needs and—just as important—whether training is the answer. Many experienced trainers say unequivocally that you should never train without having first conducted a needs analysis. This advice is sound, though the assessment might well be merely to confirm, for example, that the accidents occurring on the production line are the result of workers' not knowing how to properly use a new machine. As the situation becomes more complex, for example, if you wish to determine how to increase productivity in order to compete in a marketplace dominated by stiff international competition, needs analysis becomes key. Where major change is targeted and the stakes are high, as when an organization is adopting a totally new approach to customer service or a quality improvement program, training needs assessment can make the difference between success and failure.

The front-end analysis preceding any important management action asks a number of important questions—for example: What are the issues? What are the problems? What is going wrong that needs fixing—or what needs to be done to keep things going well? After the assessment comes the process of determining exactly what action to take.

Some people have a knack for getting in the car (not bothering with computer-generated directions and leaving the navigation system turned off), heading in the general direction they want to go, and arriving at their destination a reasonable time later, all without a map and without a hitch. Most of us, however, need the map—and not just any map. It must be one that can get us where we want to be, with the least fuss and in the shortest time. In developing training, the way to be successful is to stay focused on performance, asking, "What should the person be able to do when training is completed?"

Step Two Summary

Needs assessment is one of two training tools we can use to lay out our training road map. The other is performance objectives. Both are successfully applied by managers every day to the critical things they have to do. Important management decisions of any kind are generally not made without assessing the situation and potential outcomes beforehand. Needs assessment determines where we want to go; learning objectives act as the road map showing how to get there. Included in this step are:

- Needs assessment tools.
- Built-in analysis gauges.
- Methods of gathering information.
- Procedures for identifying learning objectives (with plenty of samples of how to develop good ones).

Needs Assessment

The needs assessment tools and examples you'll find here will likely be familiar to you because their principles are broadly applicable. One way to picture assessment is to use the analogy of paying a visit to your family physician. The doctor will ask you specific questions regarding your symptoms in order to determine what caused your ailment and what can be done to provide relief and, ultimately, a cure. If your lifestyle is contributing to the problem or if the work you do is not conducive to your good health, the doctor may suggest you do something about it—perhaps take medication, begin therapy, undergo surgery, or change the way you eat. The trainer does the same thing, looking at the symptoms—for example, low productivity, lack of work skills, or unhappy customers—and assessing which problems and conditions training can help turn around.

Purpose of Needs Assessment

The purpose of needs assessment is to identify training needs. The ultimate goal is to be able to determine whether employee performance, and thus organization performance, meets established standards.

A vital consideration is to ensure that the process sorts out the problems and concerns for which training offers a solution. Let's say a particular work crew has low productivity. Needs assessment may discover that the problem stems from a recent change in time-off policies that has affected several senior employees who stand to lose from it. In this situation, no amount of training will overcome the problem, unless it can be determined that an orientation session might pay off by helping to explain why the new policy was put into effect. Even so, the reason would have to be quite strong for training to have an impact on performance.

It's up to the trainer to do the detective work of uncovering the information needed to make a sound decision about whether training is the key to improving performance. If someone has already done such an assessment, so much the better, but make sure you agree with the established need.

Bear in mind when conducting training needs analysis that you're not likely to have enough resources, time, and funding to solve all problems (let alone conduct an exhaustive assessment). This means you must become adept at prioritizing and identify situations where the most good—that is, the most effective improvement in overall performance—will be realized by training. Realities of time and money have an impact on even the most well-staffed, dedicated, and successful training departments.

Here's a final important idea: Needs assessment is closely related to evaluation of training, the assessment done after the fact (Step Seven). When the analysis is done properly and thoroughly, it will be relatively easy to determine how well the training went: You compare what the training achieved to what you wanted it to achieve. This leads us to the next key concept of needs assessment.

Gap Analysis

If you've had the opportunity to ride the London Underground, chances are you've heard the message "Mind the gap" broadcast over the public address system just as the train pulls to a stop at the platform. It serves as a warning to boarding and leaving passengers that there's a gap between the platform and the deck of the car, so they should be careful. It's a message well worth heeding; a few train car models leave a gap large enough that a person's foot could get caught between the car and platform.

This analogy serves well for what we want to achieve with training. We want to close the gap between current skills and desired skills. The gap may be easy to see; for example, giving word processing staff keyboard lessons will speed up data entry. There may be a larger divergence, such as when a major corporate employer must move from a local market to a global one. Needs assessment is the process by which we measure how wide the gap is, which tells us how much training is needed (and, indeed, whether training can contribute to closing the gap). Exhibit 2-1 illustrates the gap analysis process and includes several examples.

Exhibit 2-1. Gap analysis.

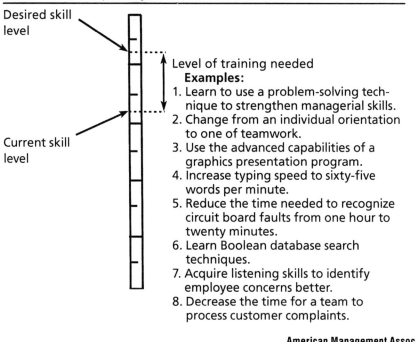

Desired skill level

Current skill level

Level of training needed
Examples:
1. Learn to use a problem-solving technique to strengthen managerial skills.
2. Change from an individual orientation to one of teamwork.
3. Use the advanced capabilities of a graphics presentation program.
4. Increase typing speed to sixty-five words per minute.
5. Reduce the time needed to recognize circuit board faults from one hour to twenty minutes.
6. Learn Boolean database search techniques.
7. Acquire listening skills to identify employee concerns better.
8. Decrease the time for a team to process customer complaints.

American Management Association
www.amanet.org

Four Ways to Keep Focused on Purpose

Determining training needs is a vital front-end process, and it takes time to accomplish. We must quickly get to the business of why training is needed in order to complete the front-end steps and get down to conducting the training. Staying focused on the issue at hand is crucial to effective and efficient needs analysis. Here are four important reminders for you to keep in front of you as you determine needs and verify the purpose of the training you are to conduct. They're summarized in Exhibit 2-2.

Exhibit 2-2. Four ways to keep focused on the purpose of training.

1. *Focus on problems training can solve.* There's nothing more frustrating than wasting time applying training to a lost cause. It also wastes two important commodities: time and money.
2. *Focus on what is and what should be; then figure out how training can close the gap.* Here you use a simple tool: gap analysis. This is nothing more than common sense—the sort of thing people do all the time to improve situations.
3. *Focus on how to improve performance.* This will keep you on track and help you comply with the first two ways, while improving talent levels of trainees. This is what separates successful trainers from the pack.
4. *Focus on simplicity.* This is the stuff that keeps people out of trouble, holds costs down, makes bosses and people receiving the training happy, and makes you, the trainer, successful.

1. *Focus on problems that training can solve.* Everything else is a waste of your time, is a problem for someone else to solve, or requires techniques and actions other than training. For example, if the circumstances point to conflicting policies within an organization that contribute to an identified business problem, training will not solve the problem, no matter how much is conducted. What's needed is a change of policy. If a breakdown in production stems from the fact that employees don't know the details of the policy, training might help—or perhaps merely restating the policy in clear terms and effectively communicating it might work. Another possibility is to develop a new policy and conduct

a short training session to indoctrinate staff on how to implement it. The point to keep in mind is this: Training must be a prime candidate to resolve the issue under scrutiny.

2. *Focus on what is and what should be; then figure out how training can close the gap.* It's not enough to determine what the problem is—for example, that supervisors aren't doing a good job of listening to their subordinates. You must also determine such matters as how important listening is, how much attention you want the supervisors to pay to their workers, and so on. Your aim is to provide the amount of training—neither too much nor too little—that achieves the level of improvement and change desired.

   You might not be able to close the entire gap at once. In that case, implement a phased training approach, solving part of the problem and then taking another look. Let's say you are installing a completely new information system in your company. Trying to get employees up to speed on all aspects of it at once could easily be overwhelming to them.

3. *Focus on how to improve performance.* Performance is the name of the game. Needs assessment must determine whether you are tasked with making an improvement to solve a problem. If there is no problem, then determine whether productivity can be increased in order to meet competitive demands. Perhaps you need to do both. The point is that needs assessment must first establish the level of performance being achieved now and then define, as precisely as possible, how much improvement is to be made. We hear a lot about performance these days—performance management, pay for performance, team performance, and performance systems, to name a few—and for good reason. This is no mere buzzword or hot-ticket item. It's real and has a direct impact on the bottom line. Effective performance is what separates success from failure. As corporations downsize in troubled times (and sometimes in not so troubled ones), performance becomes even more critical when you have fewer people performing.

4. *Focus on simplicity.* When a problem is bearing down on an organization, taking time to conduct a needs assessment is a luxury that is not an option. This is true even if there's a generous budget. Simplicity provides the guiding light in the continuing challenge of balancing such factors as time and resources against needs assessment. Simplicity in this context means:

American Management Association
www.amanet.org

- Making note of any problems that have turned up that you
  cannot solve through training and moving on to those that
  training can resolve
- Resisting the temptation to solve too many problems at once
  (i.e., prioritizing)
- Determining whether there's a reasonable training solution
  (in other words, don't try to take on a major training challenge you know you won't get funding for, even if training is
  the obvious answer)
- Refraining from making the needs you identify fit predetermined solutions (e.g., training packages you've heard about
  from a colleague or read about in a professional journal)
- Reducing identified needs to their lowest common denomi-
  nator (e.g., it isn't enough to determine that there's a drop in
  productivity; dig enough to find out why)
- Making sure that all needs you identify are clear to everyone
  who will need to deal with them

Common sense and a solid grounding in problem-solving
techniques—the sort of thing managers do every day—will stand
the needs analyst in good stead (see Step One).

Organizational Factors That Lead to Need for Training

Much of the work of trying to figure out whether training is needed
can be met by taking a look at what is occurring within the organization. Some workplace issues and events automatically require that
training be conducted (e.g., installation of a new computer network).
Following are several common situations and events where training is often required: when the company is seeking performance
improvement, quality improvement, or improvements in workplace
safety; when there have been promotions and advancement of personnel; when the company is dealing with new markets or new
people; when there are problems to solve; or when the company is
facing new technology, new laws, or organizational change. It's an
extensive list, one that can assist you in anticipating future training
needs. Here are some additional thoughts on these situations:

- *Performance Improvement.* There are many ways to determine
  whether performance can be improved through training. One

way to look at it is that there's always a need to improve; the question is whether training investment will yield an adequate return on investment. Improved performance, as we know, keeps organizations competitive and ultimately successful, and it's what many of us must do to advance—possibly even to keep our job. But there are also indicators, both quantitative and qualitative, such as quarterly production figures and weekly sales reports. Common sense prevails here, since it's the manager's job to know if performance is where it should be.

- *Quality Improvement.* This can come about for several reasons: a desire to move into a position of providing a higher level of service than the competition; an increase in the number of products that customers return; an alliance with other companies in a global marketplace where international quality assurance standards are required (e.g., European companies),

- *Safety Issues.* The best way to think of training for safety is in the positive sense: heading off problems before they occur by keeping a close eye on areas where safety is paramount and determining whether the safety level is where it should be. For example, periodic safety review sessions might help keep workers alert to potential problems. The other side of this coin is to look at safety numbers to determine whether they're unacceptable. If the accident rate for drivers is going up, a refresher training session might be in order. There's a close correlation between safety and training, so this is one area to review continually for possible training needs.

- *Promotions and Advancement.* Executive succession planning is a serious organization concern. Also, where skills are in short supply, the need to be ready to replace key workers may receive a lot of executive attention. One of the main things employees look for on the job is the ability to move up in the organization. Training is relevant to these situations. New responsibilities often require new skills that training can provide.

- *New Markets and New Lines of Business.* Many companies are finding that they need to do more than enter new markets; they may have to redefine themselves in order to undertake completely new lines of business. This is a fact of today's competitive marketplace and affects the nonprofit sector, as well. Sometimes the solution is to redefine what the business is, such as changing the product or service from computers to information or from trucking to transportation. Whatever the nature of the change, training may be essential for a number of reasons—for example, to learn about the new marketplace or product, to prepare marketing staff on how to market in a new environment, or to train production and service staff to produce and maintain the new product or service.

- *New Employees.* Anytime new staff members come on board, there's need for training. They may need particular skills, or perhaps new supervisors must be trained to handle the expanded staff. Even if the new staff members have the desired skills (which could be the reason they were hired), they need orientation to the new place of business. Most companies claim they conduct orientation training, but often this is little more than a brief session to show new staff where the coffee machine and rest rooms are located. Orientation is more; it means acquainting people with what the organization is all about—its mission, culture, and expectations, including performance expectations. This is particularly important when you consider that a young person entering the workplace today can expect to work for many different organizations during the course of a career.

- *Problem Solving.* Problem solving has made its way from the boardroom down to the lowest levels of organizations as downsizing, flattening, and empowering are put into place. Training is the best way to prepare people to deal with new problems and new challenges. If teams are involved, the need for training may be critical to enable teams to function effectively. Firsthand experience is good, but it is made much better when it is put into a training context. In fact, problem-solving training—training people how to use tried-and-true problem-solving techniques—is a much-used and successful training application.

- *New Technology, Systems, or Procedures.* Technology has a way of providing solutions to one set of problems (e.g., decreasing time spent in responding to customer queries), while creating new ones (e.g., causing people to scramble to learn how to use the new technology). A common tendency is to install new technology, different systems, or new procedures for getting work done while neglecting to train people in how to use it to its best advantage. A simple rule to follow is this: When acquiring new technology, provide the training that people need to be able to use it in the most effective way. Sometimes this can be a simple matter of including a video training package with the purchase of a new piece of software, training built into the software, or engaging vendor trainers. Similarly, when implementing new ways of doing things—whether converting to a team- and customer-oriented workplace (a major change) or simply changing the way purchases are to be made—make sure the employees who will be affected by the change can properly use the new system or procedure—*before* it has to be used. More often than not, this means that training will be needed. Front-end training will likely be less costly than lost productivity or effectiveness due to lack of skills.

- *New Laws.* Anytime a new workplace-related law is enacted, it's not a bad idea to assume that you need to conduct training up front on how to comply with it—for example, by bringing in an expert to explain to everyone affected by it how to avoid problems. It may be necessary to weigh the cost of training against the potential cost of having employees continue to function without knowing how to comply. Considering the number of human resources, civil rights, safety, and other laws that affect the workplace, this is an area worth paying attention to.
- *Organization Change.* This is closely related to the category of new technology, systems, and procedures. When a company seeks to change the way it goes about conducting its business, employees must be ready to conduct business in the new way immediately. Usually, training is needed, possibly before the change takes place. The success of such massive organization changes as the implementation of quality programs, customer service orientation, and new teams or other new organization forms is heavily dependent on training. Corporate mergers magnify the need for organizational change training.

Types of Needs Assessment

There are a number of ways to conduct needs analysis. The steps learned in engineering school or in a problem-solving or decision-making course will serve quite well. Common sense used in making important personal decisions will also work. Your intuition and experience may lead you quickly to what will work best for your situation. Commonly used types of needs assessments are task and skill analysis, focus groups, critical incidents, and performance reviews. (Exhibit 2-3 gives some examples of when to use these types of needs assessment.)

Exhibit 2-3. When to use selected types of needs assessment.

Types of Needs Assessment	Potential Applications.
Task and skill analysis	Adding new technology (e.g., a new management information system)
	Creating new positions
	Redefining jobs
	Cross-training for teams
Focus groups	Solving organization problems
	Implementing new projects, contracts, or products
Critical incidents	Reviewing processes and activities for potential training needs
	Observing after changes have been made
Performance review	Checking performance
	Checking for training needs
Anticipating need for training	Reviewing processes and activities Monitoring for safety

Task and Skill Analysis

This process is useful when a new system is being installed, and operator functions are now different, possibly even totally new; for example, perhaps a fully automated manufacturing system is set to replace an older system. In this case, there are likely no workers who can operate the new system. Task and skill analysis can also be used to assess processes such as planning or budgeting that can be broken down into discrete actions.

To illustrate how to perform a task and skill analysis, consider a company that is upgrading its data-based management system to a customized version with considerably more capabilities than the old one. To perform the analysis, you will need to work with technical experts, including designers and programmers, on how to operate the new system. Instructional information, including manuals, on-line help, and job aids, will be a big help.

There are six steps to follow in conducting task and skills analysis:

1. *Identify the job(s) or process* (e.g., word-processor operator, maintenance technician, planner).

2. *Break the job (or process) into its major tasks* (e.g., initializing the computer and word-processing software package, typing and editing documents, managing files, printing, and so on).
3. *Break each task into subtasks* (e.g., formatting documents might include formatting lines, pages, and documents, and other capabilities such as turning systems on and off, down to the step-by-step requirements for using the system).
4. *Identify all tasks and subtasks*, using appropriate terminology from the package and listing them on worksheets, with a separate one for each task, and also listing subtasks.
5. *Identify skills required to perform each task and subtask* (e.g., typing, initializing the computer, initializing the word-processing program).
6. *Determine which tasks and skills are subject to training* (e.g., if workers already know how to use the computer, it isn't necessary to provide training on initializing the system).

Exhibit 2-4 shows a sample breakdown for a task and skill analysis and illustrates a format that can be used.

Exhibit 2-4. Sample task and skill analysis worksheet.

Job/Function: Word Processor_____ Analyst_____ Date_____

Task/Description	Steps	Frequency/Systems/ Resources
Formatting a document:	1. Margins	PC
	2. Line spacing	Word processing application
	3. Font selection	User's manual (online)
	4. Tabulation	
	5. Graphics	
	6. Columns	
	7. Headers/footers	
	8. Justification	
Skills required:	• Touch typing	
	• Windows operating system	
	• Familiarity with icons and formatting	
	• Adeptness at using mouse	
	• Knowledge of business correspondence	

Task and skill analysis is a time-consuming and potentially expensive process, so there must be a definite reason to use it. When the need arises, though, it's a method that will ensure obtaining the desired results.

Focus Groups

Focus groups (also called task forces and tiger teams) have been used with great success to deal with a variety of situations. The scenario may be as exciting as taking on a major new project or solving a critical workplace problem. Calling together a small team of people who have the knowledge, skills, and motivation to resolve the issue, relying on their ability to analyze and identify needs and possibly solutions, pays dividends on the time spent together. The old saying about two heads being better than one is confirmed by focus groups.

For training needs analysis, there's no better way to determine precisely what the problem is and what might be done than by getting the right people together with the collective purpose of improving the situation. Identify people in the organization who are known for their analytical ability and include them. Affected representatives from outside the organization, such as customers or suppliers, can join the group, too. Using outside expertise may be cost-effective, particularly if technology and complex systems are involved.

The process starts with the person who has called the group together describing the situation in a clearly defined problem statement and providing all available information. The group then focuses on the causes of the problem and, after deliberation, identifies potential solutions. A focus group's purpose can just as easily be proactive—maybe to analyze how to improve a situation, such as worker productivity; to implement new processes and procedures for doing business; or to simplify processes and procedures. The ideal, we know, is to be so effective that serious problems never arise in the first place—and, even better, so that the competition stays in a far distant second place.

Brainstorming and consensus-building techniques may prove worthwhile for some problems, particularly complex ones.

Brainstorming is the process of asking a group of people to identify potential solutions without making judgments about them. It has been used extensively, and successfully, to identify workable ideas and solutions. Here is the process:

1. Identify the problem or issue at hand for which ideas and solutions are needed.
2. Ask each member of a group to quickly generate as many ideas or solutions as possible.
3. Record all ideas. Judgment is completely suspended.
4. Go through the list upon completion to select potentially useful items.

In *consensus building,* a group of experts is assembled and asked to go through a process that will result in consensus regarding a solution to a problem, an action, or a position to take on an issue or other appropriate topic on which agreement is sought. Here is the process:

1. Present a list of ideas or solutions (or have the group generate its own).
2. Discuss the pros and cons of each item.
3. Have members express their choices (e.g., by voting or applying predetermined weighting factors).
4. Review the results, eliminating items that the group agrees does not offer the best practice.
5. Have members repeat their selection based on the resulting list, and generate the next version of the list.
6. Repeat the process until there is agreement on the solution.

Note that the group of experts does not need to be assembled in one place for this process.

Critical Incidents

Critical incidents—those that contribute, positively or negatively, toward achieving goals and objectives—provide a convenient and meaningful source of training analysis information. The principle is that specific events that occur on the job have a major impact on determining organization effectiveness. System breakdowns, urgent customer requests, and major milestones (such as a product delivery date or an excessive number of accidents) are examples of critical incidents.

Prior to implementing this method, identify critical incidents so that they can be readily distinguished from everyday incidents. Other incidents can be added at the time they happen. The incidents can be at a departmental, team, process, or individual level. Once this is done, the remaining steps are relatively easy to complete:

1. Establish record-keeping guidelines and the media where critical incidents are to be kept (e.g., work log, supervisor notes, online).
2. Assign responsibility for maintaining the records.
3. From time to time, analyze the records to determine which incidents detracted from organization effectiveness and which did not (or possibly which ones contributed positively), the reasons for their occurring, and what can be done to resolve the negative ones and what can be learned from the positive ones to make performance even better. At this point a focus group could take over.

Performance Reviews

Since the goal of training is to improve performance, reviewing the performance of individuals or a group is a potential method of needs analysis. The exact method of reviewing performance depends on the circumstances and objectives desired. For instance, one might review the results of a department's annual performance appraisals and looking for shortfalls that could be resolved through training. Obviously, pertinent information must be available, such as a record of productivity over a period of time or a log of customer complaints. The important point is to make sure the performance review looks at the desired improvement.

A highly desirable way to conduct performance reviews is to use the existing performance management and appraisal system, simply identifying needed training on the basis of poor performance, as well as areas where growth will lead to advancement. Several key points are worth keeping in mind when reviewing performance:

1. Use clear, agreed-on standards as the baseline.
2. Focus on desired performance.
3. Accurately note actual performance.
4. Determine the causes of the lack of desired performance levels.
5. Decide whether training can facilitate achieving the desired performance.

Anticipating the Need for Training

The best way to avoid problems is to head them off. In other words, stop them before they start. This philosophy permeates proactive organizations that continually look for change that will keep them competitive. A quick review of the factors leading to a need for training earlier in this step will make it evident that many of these factors, and maybe all of them, can be anticipated and dealt with before problems occur—for example:

1. Continually scan performance to identify potential improvement areas, and continually train to keep raising the levels of output.
2. Identify areas where safety or other issues are causing problems in similar businesses or industries, and institute training to keep such problems from happening to your company.
3. Have a standing program to train people for advancement and provide orientation for newcomers.
4. Make training a built-in part of any new acquisition of technology or any new policy, procedure, or other change that is implemented.

A strong inclination for training, as identified in the concept of the learning organization (see Step Three), can go a long way toward reducing the amount of new needs assessment that must be done.

Sources of Needs Assessment Information

When deciding how to gather information for a needs analysis, keep three thoughts in mind:

1. *Chances are that you won't get too much information, if only because of time constraints.* Be selective, but remember that you'll be better off having too much information than too little. It's much easier to filter or ignore data than it is to have to search for more.
2. *Two sources are usually better than one.* The second validates the first and might turn up new, useful information. (Of course, you might not have enough time to go to more than one source.)
3. *The closer you get to the source, the better.* If customers are unhappy, meet with them; if production quality is lacking, go to the people who manufacture the products.

Though you can be innovative in seeking out information, there are five traditionally established information-gathering methods and sources: observation, data analysis, interviews, questionnaires and surveys, and instruments. As you implement one or more of these information-gathering methods, keep some questions in mind:

- What is the job?
- How is the job accomplished?
- How can job performance be improved?
- How can the skills, knowledge, and motivations required for the job be learned in the shortest time? (For problematic situations, substitute the word *incident* or *problem* for *job*.)

Observation

The best way to find out how well someone is performing is to observe. You can see for yourself how many steps an employee uses to perform the computer-aided design of a circuit board and how well the software package performs. An observer should be able to pick up any problems in the way work is performed by watching what goes on.

The first step in using observation techniques is to determine precisely what information is needed, then to decide whom to observe in order to obtain it. You may need the help of a technical or functional expert at times. If there's a quality problem, for instance, observe two or three workers considered to be at the lower end of the performance spectrum and two or three deemed to be at the upper end. A comparison of the two sets of observations will help identify potential solutions.

Answering the question of what to observe is an important one. When in doubt, expand the desired range of data points. Integral to the observation method of data gathering is a way to record the data. Visions of old-fashioned time-and-motion studies, complete with clipboards and stopwatches, come to mind, and in fact, this may be what's needed. Direct entry of information into laptop computers may simplify and speed up the process. Videotape and audiotape recorders can capture information and relevant thoughts.

One of the greatest drawbacks to observation is that people being observed are conscious of it. Thus, it's possible they'll perform differently knowing that someone is watching each movement. This close scrutiny may produce better or worse performance than usual and significantly skew the results. Being as unobtrusive as possible and conducting more than one observation will help alleviate this situation. Again, all this must be weighed against time available.

For people who do much or all of their work online, observation becomes essentially automated, because useful performance information can be extracted automatically.

Data Analysis

Along with the proliferation of computers as everyday workplace tools has come a close companion: an explosion of data. More powerful computers generate ever greater quantities of data—even an incomprehensible amount of data. Fortunately, powerful software analysis packages provide the means of easily manipulating the data. This technique is applicable when there are enormous amounts of data to work with, such as productivity records. A computer workstation is capable of keeping tabs on virtually everything the employee sitting at the keyboard does during a workday. The fact that so many processes are automated—manufacturing, communications, information, and paper handling—makes this a potentially valuable source of information.

Interviews

Interviews can be either *formal*—sessions during which the same questions are asked of all interviewees, using a standard format—or *informal*—open-ended sessions in which the interviewer has wide discretion in deciding what information to obtain. Even information interviews need to be at least partially structured to achieve consistency of data.

Here are steps to follow in conducting interviews as a needs analysis information-gathering technique:

1. Identify exactly what information is desired (but don't rule out the possibility of discovering additional, revealing facts—a potential of open-ended interviews).
2. Identify who is to be interviewed and how many people you'll need to talk to.
3. Prepare interview guidelines and, if necessary, interview worksheets, which contribute to consistency of data, even for informal interviews.

4. Brief the interviewers; train them if they're new to the process of interviewing.
5. Conduct the interviews (conduct practice ones first if necessary and if time permits).
6. Compile and analyze the results.

Records Review

This may be one of the easiest methods of data gathering. Workplace records, schedules, work logs, purchase orders, progress reports, statistical analyses, manufacturing job travelers, injury reports, recorded telephone information logs (written logbooks as well as records of voice mail, e-mail, text messages, and others), numerical records, and any other recorded information—both digital and the hard-copy variety (which still hasn't disappeared as predicted)—may provide insight needed for analysis. Information from these sources also may be subject to data analysis. Scanners and related software provide a way to capture handwritten and other information and digitize it.

Questionnaires and Surveys

When it's necessary to gather information from numerous sources (e.g., all purchasing agents in a large organization with multiple locations), surveying them, by mail, fax, e-mail, or telephone or in person, will yield the necessary information. Having a carefully prepared worksheet for the respondents to fill out (or for the surveyor to complete) when interviews are done in person or by electronic means will facilitate the process and ensure that replies are consistent. This can work the same as an interview during which the interviewer fills in a questionnaire using information obtained from the interviewee.

As with the other data-gathering methods, it's mandatory to identify what information is needed before constructing the survey form. Once this is done, the questions must be stated in terms everyone will clearly comprehend. Here is the process for building an effective questionnaire:

1. Make a list of things you want to find out—perhaps the issues that created the need for the analysis or a list generated by brainstorming.

2. Turn the list of things, or items, into questions. (See Steps Six and Seven on questioning techniques for additional information.)

3. Lay out the questionnaire. If you can obtain everything you need by having respondents merely check a yes or no box, then do it this way. The simpler and easier to complete, the better. Other formats, such as having the respondent choose one of five choices in a range (e.g., strongly agree to strongly disagree), ranked questions, and open-ended questions, also work well in particular circumstances. It's a good idea, regardless of format, to allow people the option to add their own comments. You never know what you might find out this way, and, too, people like having this option.

4. Edit the questionnaire with the audience in mind, and put it into final form. By keeping in mind the viewpoint of the potential respondents, including taking into consideration terminology they are familiar with, you make it more likely that the survey will accomplish its purpose. At all times keep in mind the potential diversity of the audience—languages spoken, age differences, educational differences, and so on—which can make a difference in how questions are answered.

5. Have others review the questionnaire and make comments. The reviewers might include someone who is an expert in the area under investigation and definitely should include someone from the intended responding audience.

6. Conduct a pilot run with the questionnaires using a small number of respondents, and evaluate the results. Choose the sample respondents from the group to be surveyed on a broad scale so that the responses will be valid (unless there's extensive revision).

7. Revise the form as needed.

8. Conduct the survey.

It may be possible to find existing survey forms for standard purposes, such as evaluation forms. However, it's likely a questionnaire will have to be developed for your specific purpose or else combined with or derived from an existing one.

Instruments

Instruments can be thought of as highly specialized questionnaires. Whereas questionnaires are designed to obtain straightforward data, instruments are more sophisticated, perhaps designed to determine how ready a group is for a training program or how resistant (or susceptible) a group is to organization change that's being planned. Other instruments are used for assessing individual leadership styles, learning styles, and personality types. There are numerous commercially available instruments. It's important to know that a great deal of expertise is needed to select the proper instrument and implement it effectively, so care must be used when selecting and executing them. (See Step Six for further discussion of instruments as a tool for delivering training.)

Performance Objectives

Successful businesspeople long ago learned that having a plan—a clear goal or objective and a way to achieve it—is the only way to ensure success. That same principle holds for training. Learning objectives, also called *performance* or *behavioral objectives*, provide the road map to success in training. If you are required to give a project update to your manager, you have a clear-cut objective: to make sure the manager goes away with the information needed to make intelligent decisions regarding your project. It's easy to see how important objectives are for a three-day training workshop, which can eat up thousands of labor hours and thousands of dollars to prepare and deliver. Objectives are also critical for training delivered online. Such training is expensive, and you don't want employees scattered around the globe wasting their time online on ineffective training. Objectives provide the insurance that people's time will be well spent. Since people and organizations tend to be goal oriented (we like to have something to shoot for), learning objectives fit in well with our work ethic.

Your Road Map to Success

The concept of learning objectives as the trainer's road map is not complicated: Achieve the objectives, and training is successful. Of greater importance is that work will improve accordingly. It's that basic. Of course, there's a catch: You have to have a proper set of learning objectives. The secret is to write them as soon as you've completed the needs assessment and before you start designing the training. They thus serve a dual purpose: They act as a road map to designing, developing, and delivering effective training and also as the learner's road map to completing the training course successfully. A third purpose is that of showing the training evaluator what to look for.

Here are some rules to follow in developing learning objectives:

1. *Be precise.* The learner is the ultimate person who must meet the objective and must easily grasp what's intended. (And bear in mind learner diversity.)
2. *Use action words.* Performance is action.
3. *Keep the objectives simple.* This can never be said often enough.
4. *Use measurable objectives.* Performance on the job must be measurable in order to determine the degree of success for the person and organization.
5. *Ensure that the measurements fit the situation.*
6. *Keep objectives to a minimum.* For each module or lesson of training (e.g., a one-hour session), have a reasonably small number of objectives.
7. *Turn the desired skills into objectives.* There's a direct relationship between the skills desired and learning objectives.
8. *Keep in mind the direct relationship between the items identified as needing training during the needs assessment and the learning objectives.* (This is virtually the same as skills desired.)

The Parts of a Learning Objective

Learning specialists tell us that a learning objective must have three parts in order to be complete and usable: performance, condition, and standard. Ideally, each objective should contain all three parts. Nevertheless, it's possible initially to identify the performance only, then later add standards and conditions. The danger of doing this is that it can turn out to be difficult to identify conditions or standards that fit the performance, making that aspect less useful.

We will examine all three parts here, but keep in mind that some situations, particularly ones where time is in short supply, may dictate that you stop with the performance. Also, conditions and standards may be uniform for all parts of the learning process and thus all the objectives. Use your judgment here, but at least develop sound performances for your objectives.

Performance

What skills, knowledge, or attitudes do you want the learner to go home with? What's expected? What behavior is to be changed? Is the trainee to learn to operate a bulldozer, plan a team meeting, generate a message over multiple transmission sources, or provide the rules to follow for safe disposal of hazardous waste? If the training has been well thought out, meaning that a careful needs assessment has been conducted, the objectives will literally leap out at you. This is the key part of the objective, the one that must *always* be present.

Condition

This part of the objective deals with the condition under which the learner must perform the objective. It may be a simulated environment (flight simulator), for example, or the actual workplace circumstance (actual aircraft). For knowledge objectives, it may be that the trainee can use references while performing the task, or perhaps this is not allowed. The condition may be an extreme situation, such as an emergency, or it may reflect a routine situation that simulates the everyday workplace. For a pilot undergoing emergency landing training in a flight simulator, the conditions are those generated by the simulator (which can be exceptionally realistic). For knowledge-related objectives, such as retrieving a particular piece of information for a planning decision, the conditions will be related to the resources that are available, such as planning tools and databases. Often the training environment—a classroom, simulator, online, or role play—is itself the condition. The condition includes any tools, equipment, documents, aids, and systems that may be required.

Standard

How well do you want the learner to perform the objective? The standard can be anywhere from performing a task a little bit better to achieving perfection. Is perfection the goal, or is plus or minus 10 percent accuracy sufficient? Think in terms of quantifiable items, such as percentages and time, or cost, or quality-related criteria, such as perfection or something less. It's the standard that ultimately provides the "grade" for the learner's performance. Representative samples of learning objectives are shown in Exhibit 2-5.

Exhibit 2-5. Sample learning objectives.

1. State the five major steps in a Six Sigma process (performance) verbatim (standard), from memory (condition).
2. After reading a case study (condition) that illustrates a Six Sigma process, identify which of the steps were applied in the case (performance), without leaving out any steps (standard).
3. Demonstrate the correct technique for performing CPR (performance) using "Annie" (condition) for five minutes (standard).
4. Type sixty-five words per minute (performance) without any mistakes (standard), using a standard keyboard (condition).
5. Develop three satisfactory learning objectives for the introductory module of a stress management training course (performance), using *The First-Time Trainer* (condition), in thirty minutes (standard).
6. Parallel-park a four-door sedan within the lines of a parking space (performance) on a public street during peak traffic (condition), within three minutes and without having to back up more than three times (standard).
7. Demonstrate the proper response to an improper sexual advance (performance) during a role play (condition) in a manner that fits within stated company policy (condition).
8. Shut down the assembly line (performance) during a simulated equipment malfunction (condition) within five seconds after the alarm sounds (standard).
9. Generate a budget for the planning department (performance) that meets the company's stated budget submission requirements (standard), using a spreadsheet application program (condition).
10. After viewing a video clip (condition), identify potential violations of the Americans with Disabilities Act (performance) and categorize the level of severity of each using the company policy guidelines (standard).

Writing the Objectives

Remember that one of the key rules for writing good objectives is to use action words. A good way to apply this rule is to ask yourself how you will measure the objective if a particular word is used. For example, the word *understand* is commonly used in training and education. Does a learner *understand* why the company is adopting a team approach to production? Does a manager *understand* why key people must be included in certain strategic decision-making situations? But how do you measure understanding? When you think about it, *understand* might better be stated as being able to identify certain facts and conditions or stating reasons that an action was taken. By contrast, the ability to compute a solution to a statistical problem or identify and write the company's long-range goals is definitely measurable.

Here are examples of action words that are acceptable and unacceptable in writing learning objectives:

Acceptable Action Words

mark	name	install
state	fix	decide
identify	move	check
fill out	place	say
label	draw	ask
perform	operate	list
compare	load	fabricate
locate	quote	prepare
maneuver	repair	demonstrate
diagnose	run	build

Unacceptable Action Words

understand	conclude	know
discover	grasp	become
enjoy	infer	believe
think	solve	improve
develop	determine	appreciate
analyze	test	

Note that some of these words could be on either list. *Test* might be a perfectly good word for an objective in a training session on how to administer training tests. *Analyze* might be just fine for a course in strategic planning. Obviously, there would have to be more explanation of what's required, such as "analyze using a prescribed technique." Generally, though, the cleaner and easier to measure, the better. Some words, such as *understand*, can never be measured.

Step Three

Focus on Learning

"What one knows is, in youth, of little moment; they know enough who know how to learn."

—Henry Brooks Adams, *The Education of Henry Adams*, 1907

Knowing how people learn is critical to effective training delivery. Since we're dealing with adults, this means applying adult learning theory. It's not difficult, because adults have a good idea of how they learn best. Just follow a few principles and practices, and learners will be enthusiastic about the process—and they'll learn more too.

Step Three Summary

This step deals with how people learn. A development that has come of age in the past few decades is an increased knowledge of how organizations learn. Step three is closely related to learning objectives, which are directly tied to performance. It includes these elements:

- The relationship between learning and motivation
- Identification of the types of learning
- Principles of learning, centered around adult learning theory
- Building learning principles into training
- Key concepts of core competency and mastery
- Learning how to learn

American Management Association
www.amanet.org

- Knowledge about the multiple ways of acquiring skills and knowledge
- Creating a learning organization
- Building success factors into the training during design
- Knowledge about why this phase is so critical to training success

This step begins with a discussion of the critical relationship between learning and motivation. It identifies types of learning, followed by a presentation of sixteen principles of learning that center around adult learning theory. Learning principles go hand in hand with learning objectives. Many of the learning principles addressed in this step are directly tied to objectives, which are tied to performance. Clearly the training-learning process is a closed-loop system.

Several concepts related to learning must be considered to ensure that the process is properly built into training. These include core competency and mastery, learning how to learn, multiple ways of acquiring skills and knowledge, and the learning organization. These factors are discussed following learning principles. Another consideration during this early design phase is addressed: the technique of building success factors into the training during design. The step concludes with a reminder of why the phase is so critical to training success.

The Learning Process

Thanks to trainers and teachers, we've learned a lot about how people learn. The result is a number of sound principles and guidelines for the trainer to follow.

Learning and Motivation

People learn for a reason. It may be positive or negative, for pleasure or survival. To say it another way, people are motivated to learn, and motivation plays a major role in the training and learning process. Acquiring new skills through training may well be the way to meet personal needs. At a basic level, the motivation to work may arise from the need to pay the rent and food bills. At a higher level, people may become fully engrossed in work so they can move to the highest levels of the organization, fulfilling their dreams of making it to the top.

There's a direct relationship between motivation and two major trainer concerns. One is that the more motivated trainers are, the more successful training will be. The other is that adult learning theory is founded on concepts of motivation. In summary, learners must be motivated if training is to be successful, and trainers must be motivated to perform well as facilitators and to continually improve performance. This dual motivation is the best route to success.

Motivation to perform after training by applying the newly acquired skills may well be the most important manifestation of motivation. For example, there may be opportunities for promotion or increased rewards based on increased skills, increased productivity, or overall improved organization performance. It isn't necessary to delve into motivational theories, but it's important to recognize that the desire most people have to better themselves and get involved with meaningful work certainly is relevant to training. These are the same motivational principles managers apply to improve organization effectiveness.

Types of Learning

Learning psychologists have provided a straightforward, easily accepted classification of learning types: knowledge, skills, and attitude. These have been widely accepted in education and training and provide a convenient means of organizing training.

Knowledge Learning

Also called *cognitive learning*, knowledge learning entails using knowledge and mental skills—for example, identifying key steps in the decision-making process, identifying marketing challenges on the basis of market analysis data, or stating the rules of the nautical road for a sailboat overtaking a motorized ship. It ranges, for example, from being able to state the three parts of a learning objective to describing in detail the underlying reasons that expert systems can be used to corporate advantage. You may have heard the term *cognitive,* or *cognitive domain*, referring to memory and reasoning objectives. This form of learning goes together with such concepts as the knowledge-driven workplace, the learning organization, and other aspects of learning (all discussed in this step). Knowledge learning examples include learning and applying rules, identifying symbols and patterns, making decisions, recalling bodies of knowledge, and applying knowledge.

Skills Learning

Also called *kinesthetic* or *psychomotor skills learning*, this is the skill type that comes to mind when we think about teaching a person the physical skills needed to perform a task: performing gross and fine motor skills, exercising eye-hand coordination, steering and maneuvering, operating, manipulating, and communicating, among others. Learning to use a keyboard to do word processing is skills learning, as is learning to use a keyboard to play music, to operate an entertainment system, or to install a new muffler in an automobile. Many physical skills are straightforward and easy to categorize—for example, operating a lathe or driving a car. Because of the growing reliance on knowledge, however, more and more skills require both physical dexterity and knowledge skills.

Attitude Learning

Also called *affective learning,* this is related to values and interests; examples are taking a wallet full of money to the lost and found, being ethical in dealing with customers, adopting the *Semper Fi* attitude of a U. S. Marine, or working overtime with no regrets in order to meet a deadline. This is where our deep concern for corporate ethics comes into play. A person's emotional capacity and individual objectives related to personal feelings and values also play an important role in attitude learning.

It isn't always possible to separate these three kinds of learning in actual practice, even though it may be possible for training purposes. For example, a word-processor operator must have certain knowledge before being able to apply physical skills in manipulating the keyboard. The pianist must have knowledge of notes and chords before playing a melody from memory in front of a concert audience. And having the desire to perform the various skills to the absolute best of one's ability, which is attitude, can make a world of difference to the person and the organization—and the audience, in the case of the pianist.

Learning Principles

Learning theory is a major field of study, with an extensive body of knowledge. Learning psychologists continue to supply research on how to facilitate the learning process. It's exciting that we continue to learn more about how the brain works and how this knowledge might someday help trainers better focus on the learning process. The theory is based on sound, field-tested principles. Because of this immense body of work, trainers don't have to worry about research and theory. We can feel quite safe in simply applying the principles. It helps that most of them are already familiar to most of us. All we're required to do is follow them, which over the long term will help guarantee successful training. It will also build in the motivational aspect that is so essential.

Here we look at sixteen learning principles—seven that come from adult learning theory and nine that are basic principles of how people learn. Chances are you're familiar with most, if not all, of them. When applied, they'll keep you on track toward effective training. (They are summarized in Exhibit 3-1.)

Exhibit 3-1. Sixteen learning principles for effective training.

1. *Adults learn by doing.*
2. *Use realistic examples.*
3. *Adults relate their learning to what they already know.*
4. *Conduct the training in an informal environment.*
5. *Variety is the spice of life.*
6. *Remove the fear factor.*
7. *Serve as the facilitator of the learning process.*
8. *Inform learners of the learning objectives.*
9. *Practice makes perfect.*
10. *Guide and prompt; do not tell.*
11. *Give feedback.*
12. *Apply transfer of training.*
13. *Relate all activities to the learning objectives.*
14. *Make a good first impression.*
15. *Show enthusiasm.*
16. *Use repetition.*

Note: These principles apply regardless of the delivery method. The challenge for the developer of online learning is to make sure the principles are integral to the lesson being completed, whether the trainee is a person sitting in a hotel room halfway around the world or someone sitting in a classroom.

1. *Adults learn by doing.* Adults want to be involved in whatever it is they do, particularly when learning something new. Don't demonstrate; let the adult learner do it. There's really nothing new here, because we know that getting our hands on the task—learning by doing—is what constitutes ultimate learning. Why talk about key learning points when you can let adult learners do as much of the work as possible? Be a facilitator. Not only are you more likely to succeed, but adult learners will appreciate the process more.

2. *Use realistic examples.* Use plenty of examples, and keep them realistic and relevant to learners. If you don't, the examples will be meaningless. For one reason why, look to the next item, about how adults use familiar frames of reference to enhance their learning. Along these lines, make sure the examples are interesting and attention getting so everyone enjoys the training.

3. *Adults relate their learning to what they already know.* Sometimes they do so in a pronounced way. Knowing their backgrounds and experiences will help immensely. Adults have plenty of experiences, with some being more prevalent than others. The result is that they compare the new with what they've already done and know, focusing on what they know best. The more abstract you are, the less likely it is that the learner will relate to the learning. This concept is one good reason that icebreakers (see Step Six) serve more than one purpose, including allowing the facilitator to learn more about who is being facilitated. So much the better if the information can be obtained prior to the training sessions.

4. *Conduct the training in an informal environment.* No one wants to sit through a rigid, by-the-numbers training session. This doesn't mean you can be sloppy. Informality can range from specifying informal attire, to including low-key social events with the training, to simply making everyone feel at ease at the beginning of the session.

5. *Variety is the spice of life.* Change the pace and technique in training from time to time. Use different delivery methods and

audiovisuals. Bring in other people or change the setting. This concept of multimodality is another excellent example of variety that pays dividends. (Media and delivery methods, where you can accomplish this, are discussed in Steps Five and Seven.) Exhibit 3-2 provides examples of how to use multimodality approaches in training. This is especially important if the training group consists of a mix of both younger and older learners.

Exhibit 3-2. Multimodality approaches in training.

1. Show a video on ethics, followed by an open discussion. Have learners summarize by writing out the key points they learned. You can substitute any number of topics for ethics, and the process will still work to stimulate many learning styles.

2. Give a minilecture on a three-step planned change model. Have learners read a case study; then, have them form groups and discuss how the model could be used to deal with the problem situation. Following this, have each group present its solutions.

3. Have learners read a manual on how to set up an accounting form on a spreadsheet. Demonstrate how to set it up properly (or show a video, or perhaps have a learner do the demonstration). Give learners an assignment to work on in pairs, to set up an assigned form. Have each group demonstrate its results.

4. Have learners develop their personal definition of the topic under study (e.g., what constitutes good speaking skills). Show a video clip demonstrating a good presentation (or have someone else do it). Have small groups compare observed skills with the ones they developed. Summarize by writing their findings on a board or flip chart.

5. Deliver a classroom presentation topic, such as the company's mission statement, for a new employee orientation class. Have learners look up competitor mission statements on the Internet, and compare the statements in small discussion groups. Finally, ask learners to write a paragraph on what the mission statements mean to them.

6. Show a video depicting a company where teams are used successfully. Next, have learners participate in an exercise where they must engage in teamwork to be successful. Finally, have them discuss (or write) what they see as being the keys to successful teams.

7. Use other ideas to stimulate learner senses:

American Management Association
www.amanet.org

- Add appropriate music (e.g., to announce transitions from one segment to another).
- Incorporate storytelling and drama.
- Move outdoors for exercises or go to different locations, such as actual workplaces, customers, or suppliers.
- Have people experience unique situations, such as simulating people from other cultures or persons with a disability.

6. *Remove the fear factor.* People have memories, not always happy ones, about cramming for tests and anxiously awaiting report cards and grade postings. Avoid this environment in adult training situations. (There may be times when this is impossible, as when personal safety is a critical factor.) Feedback is essential, but provide it in informal ways—and often. Praise is the best form of reward. Provide the guidance needed in a win-win situation. Note how frequently performance and performance objectives are mentioned throughout the eight steps. If a person can meet the prescribed performance laid out in training, then there probably is no need for grading. Everyone will gain more if the fear factor is removed or reduced as much as possible.

7. *Serve as the facilitator of the learning process.* Be a trainer, not a teacher. Granted, the learners probably will expect you to do some teaching. For example, if they come to the session to learn how to use a computer, some old-fashioned teaching is in order. Remember that the learners are most likely to be as accomplished in whatever it is they do as you are in what you do, so be sure to treat everyone respectfully. This principle also means that you must be flexible, quick to adapt to the situation if it means a greater chance for success.

8. *Inform the learners of the learning objectives.* It's up to you to provide the road map the learners need, checking frequently to determine whether everyone is on track to achieve the objectives. Remember from Step Two that you need a well-defined set of objectives before designing and developing training, let alone delivering it.

9. *Practice makes perfect.* Practice can bring the learner much closer to being able to achieve the desired objectives. It's a vital consideration, tied to one of the most popular, and potentially beneficial, ideas of today's workplace: competency and mastery.

Multimodality and repetition (included in the last principle in this list) provide the means of applying and reinforcing this principle.

10. *Guide and prompt; do not tell.* Learning lasts much longer when the learner has to fully enter into the learning process. Provide all the help you can by citing references, giving examples, asking questions, and offering all the encouragement you can to learners so that they will provide the answers and demonstrate the desired performance.

11. *Give feedback.* This is essential and must be done continually so that everyone knows exactly what progress has been made and how much more needs to be done.

12. *Apply transfer of training.* The principle that one aspect of learning builds on another applies to most basic skills. For example, basic arithmetic skills can be transferred to learning how to balance a checkbook, then to learning simple accounting systems. Basic computer skills can be transferred to learning how to use a spreadsheet. Day-to-day decision-making skills for supervisors can be transferred to skills for making vital management decisions. One aspect of training builds on another, a principle that can be invaluable to trainers. This is a fundamental part of learning how to learn.

13. *Relate all activities to the learning objectives.* When you conduct an exercise, for example, make sure the purpose is tied to the objectives and that the learners are aware of it. Use learning objectives to keep all training on track. The only training events that don't deal directly with learning objectives are breaks, and even these serve the purpose of keeping learners refreshed for maximum learning.

14. *Make a good first impression.* This should go without saying and is closely related to the principle of being thoroughly prepared for every training event. We form quick opinions, usually negative ones, when things get off to a bad, slow, too fast, or boring start. There's heavy competition for people's attention, and you sometimes must vie for your share.

15. *Show enthusiasm.* Consider what must be going on in the learners' minds if you're dragging through a session. If you are the least bit bored, uncertain, or unenthusiastic, learners will be

even more so. Unless you are a seasoned performer, showing enthusiasm may take a bit of extra effort. Also, make sure your body language matches your voice and expression. (At times, acting as a stand-up comedian might save the day.)

16. *Use repetition.* This is the old principle of repetition, reiteration, and rote. Repeat things three times at least, preferably in slightly different ways. Here's where the concept of multimodality comes in handy, by making repetition more interesting and exciting by doing it in different ways (e.g., telling how to manage conflict, demonstrating it, then having learners practice it in role plays).

Teaching or Training?

Is there a difference between teaching and training? At first glance, you might not think so, and, in fact, the words are often used interchangeably. Certainly there are similarities, and many people have moved successfully from education to training and development by applying similar principles. However, there are distinct differences, and no doubt those who have made the transition successfully know what they are. One of the primary differences is that training takes an adult approach to learning theory, recognizing the differences between the traditional way children learn and how adults learn. There are other differences, as well (bearing in mind that teachers can and do facilitate):

- *Knowledge.* This is largely *discovered* in training rather than passed on, as in teaching. Rather than have the teacher tell learners what the "truth" is, the trainer facilitates learners' discovery of the truth.
- *Improvement.* Teaching emphasizes technical advancement within the organization, such as installing advanced computer systems and teaching people how to use them. Training emphasizes improvement through developing the people—the human resource of the organization.
- *Orientation.* The teaching approach is oriented toward the teacher; the training approach is oriented toward the learner.
- *Behavior.* Teaching is concerned with measurable behavior. So is training, but it also cares about attitudes. Positive reinforcement is a boon to trainers.

- *Objectives.* Teaching focuses on precise behavioral objectives, emphasizing the acquisition of information. Training is also concerned with precision but adds an emphasis on interpersonal skills competencies (learning how to learn).
- *Content.* Teaching relates content to technical skills. Training adds personal skills, such as decision making and critical thinking, and some of the softer skills required in interpersonal relations, management, and leadership.
- *Methodology.* Teaching is subject oriented, perhaps emphasizing the principles toward the end of the list of sixteen learning principles, and employs the lecture approach. Training, more personalized and geared to the situation, stresses more involvement on the part of the learner.

As you can see, the trainer focuses more on the concept of the learner as a key resource of the organization. In addition, the trainer goes beyond basics.

Other Aspects of Learning

Several new concepts have emerged that have a positive impact on training and learning: core competency and mastery, new ways of learning, and the learning organization. Each can be applied to the entire process of improving individual and organization performance through training and learning, and each adds an exciting, positive dimension to training.

Core Competency and Mastery

Intense competition for markets or resources, or both, has forced organizations worldwide to pay close attention to everything they do. One of the exciting outcomes as far as trainers are concerned is the increased focus on levels of workplace competence. How competent a person is at performing a particular job is important. Put all the employees of the organization together—everyone from the newest entry-level worker to the chief executive—and you can see why the idea is so vital. Greater competence leads to greater results, and training is a viable way to reach competency.

Mastery is the highest level of competence. It's essentially the process of being the best that it is humanly possible to be at a particular job. It means more than being good at using a database management system or developing a new business model. The greatest success will be achieved by those who can create the database or write a business plan better than anyone else in the organization—perhaps anywhere else. Here are the characteristics of a master:

- *Continually Improving.* Masters are never satisfied with their achievements and fully believe they can do better. They improve through all the ways identified in Step Eight, and more.
- *Always Learning.* Masters recognize that there's always more to learn about a job. They use every way possible to learn and improve.
- *Willing to Take Risks.* Masters are willing to stick their necks out; they have full confidence that in most cases they'll succeed. Even when they fail, which is seldom, they know they'll improve from having tried.
- *Setting High Goals.* Masters aim for goals that are high enough to require them to stretch to meet them; once they have achieved these goals, masters immediately set new ones. Restlessness is a distinct characteristic of masters.
- *Willing to Try New Ways of Doing Things.* Masters recognize that trying new things can lead to better, more effective ways of doing the job. This characteristic goes hand in hand with risk taking and separates masters from those who may know one right way to accomplish a task and never deviate from it.

The organization where mastery is part of the culture has a much greater chance of succeeding in the world of learning and performance that those that do not value mastery.

Competence and mastery are the first requirement for organization success. The second requirement is identifying both individual and organization core competencies. Whereas a company might have a core competency of providing high-quality financial protection services to families, a company employee's core competency might be the ability to discern a customer's needs and to make recommendations that fit those needs. A scientist's core competency might be in applying innovative research techniques in drug research; the drug company's core competency might be in discovering cures for disease. The significance of core competency can be illustrated by noting that organizations that have identified their core competencies and stick to them are the ones most likely to succeed.

Learning principles can be integrated into competency to enhance employees' mastery of those skills needed to make the organization most effective. The key is to use core competencies to guide all training. Here is a four-step program:

1. Identify organization and individual core competencies (based on mission).
2. Place these competencies at the heart of all employee training.
3. Make mastery a fundamental concept of the organization.
4. Continually review organization objectives, core competencies, and ongoing training to ensure their alignment.

Different Ways of Learning

If you stop to think about all the different things you're capable of doing, it will likely turn out that many of them you learned on your own, without a teacher and without attending an intensive workshop. The reason is that you've learned how to learn. In fact, successful, well-trained, and well-adjusted people often, without suggestion and completely on their own, learn what they need to know to progress in a job or task.

People who have learned how to learn have two general characteristics: They have taken control of their own learning, and they have developed several key learning skills. Note that learners must have these characteristics to gain the most from online learning in particular.

Self-Control of Learning

People who have learned how to learn will learn even if their employer does absolutely nothing to help prepare them. They have a personal plan for learning and improvement laid out, and they follow it religiously. They are also likely to be quite familiar with how they learn best. For example, someone who learns best by reading makes sure there is always plenty of appropriate reading matter on the subject at hand. Hands-on learners learn from everything they come in contact with, most certainly from others around them.

They're the ones who sit in the front row during a workshop and ask plenty of insightful questions, and they are the first to volunteer to perform a demonstration or give an example. You will find that Generation Y learners definitely appreciate being able to have some degree of control over their learning environments.

Learning to Learn Skills

For all practical purposes, the key skills learners need if they are to continue learning (i.e., learning how to learn) are the same ones a student needs in moving into college and graduate programs, further emphasizing the continuing integration of learning in all aspects of life and work. The skills include these:

- Strong study habits
- Self-motivation
- Ability to use diverse information sources
- Excellent communication skills (reading, writing, speaking, listening), including familiarity with electronic means of communication
- Problem-solving ability
- Abstract thinking ability
- Plan for learning, with specific goals
- Knowledge of how they learn best (research shows that there are multiple types of human intelligence)

Note how closely these skills track the key skills identified in Step One, particularly that of information literacy, that are needed in the workplace. The higher the level of these skills that learners acquire, the more successful they'll be in achieving learning objectives.

Other Strategies in Training and Developing People

Breakthroughs in how to acquire knowledge are keeping up with new ways to apply knowledge. The result is a challenge to trainers to keep up, but it is well worth the effort because of the potential for improved training results. We look briefly at several of these concepts. You're encouraged to keep these concepts, and any new ones you are aware of, in mind as you develop your own training. They worked for others and may be what you need to put your training over the top.

Participatory Learning

If participatory forms of managing (e.g., self-directed teams, quality circles) are successfully implemented, it stands to reason that participatory forms of training are being used also—and successfully. The two go hand in hand. If the people closest to the work know best how to do it, then certainly they know best what kinds of training they need. This is empowerment at its fullest application. In the team format, for instance, it means that each team is its own training manager. Members make their own decisions about training. The concept works well when the people held responsible for a task are given the resources and knowledge to implement it.

This also accords closely with the concept that people are responsible for their own destinies; that is, the individual, not the organization, is responsible for his or her career management. In work environments where individuals, not the organization, must take control of their own development, participatory learning is the norm, with the organization providing the climate and resources for this to work well.

Practical Training

Practical training is the process of focusing on the fastest and least expensive way to get training done. Actually, it's what good trainers and managers do all the time. They combine efficiency with effectiveness. Sometimes merely developing a job aid is just as good as training, and possibly better. Safety signs placed around equipment and instructions built into copy machines are two simple, effective examples of this kind of aid. Combining an ongoing training program with actual work—on-the-job training—is another excellent example of practical training that works (see self-paced training in Step Four). This may mean that, in situations where a particular task is done only occasionally, having someone else do certain portions of a job may be the best approach. Primarily it's an attitude that borders on taking the position that training should be done only when absolutely necessary. Carefully followed, it can eliminate wasted training and wasted expense by focusing on what works best and most quickly. (Just be careful not to be too miserly.)

Action Learning

Many organizations are finding that learners who accomplish actual tasks rather than hypothetical ones during training get far more out of the process. This action learning often works well with teams. Companies that have tried this approach find that the more diverse the people on the team, the better action learning works.

How training results are measured varies when real business issues are used as the basis of training. Measurement can range from a discussion of the outcome to an assessment of results. Either way, accountability and risk are built into the process—one of the main reasons this training can be so effective. As you can see, this accords closely with much of what we've learned about how adults learn. (See Step Four on designing training and Step Six on getting learners involved for related discussion.)

Technology

Technology adds depth and versatility to training, and its application continues to increase. It should not be used simply for the sake of using it or because someone you know has used it. But where it fits and can be cost justified, use it. It contributes to realism and cuts costs in the right situations. (Specific technologies, particularly e-learning, are addressed in Step Five.)

Lifelong Learning

We never stop learning. Retired people continue to learn about many things, including acquiring technology skills. Here's where we bring together the concepts of learning how to learn, acquiring information-gathering skills, and continually updating skills to excel (sometimes to merely keep up), which are required in the knowledge-driven economy and workplace. Continuous learning is essential to success in virtually any field.

The Learning Organization

Through a new management buzzword a couple of decades ago, the concept of the learning organization has made inroads into organizations and has made a definite impact on training and development. It's the belief that organizations, like individuals, can learn and that doing so on an ongoing basis can lead to continuing organization success. A learning organization has the following characteristics:

- Learning continuously is not only encouraged but expected.
- The organization's culture provides opportunities to learn and advance.
- The organization strives to perform at the highest levels.
- Creativity and innovation are common.
- People are allowed to fail.
- New ideas are always welcome.
- Organization mission and goals are clear and made known to all. They drive daily business affairs and outside relationships.
- Teams are the norm, and people are team players.
- New skills are acquired often before they are needed.
- The organization is viewed as a system.

Obviously, the organization is learning through its people, which means that there must be an environment for learning and growing. Formal training may or may not be a fundamental element of a true learning organization, but training of some sort, albeit on the job, must be present. Chances are that training is built into the organization's daily life. Review of long-term success in companies that have survived in the world arena shows that they've been learning and growing for a long time, without bothering to name the process. Creativity, empowerment, teamwork, mastery, and the ability to adapt to rapid change are core traits of a learning organization. When the organization is conscious of the need for continued learning, overall training has an even greater impact on effectiveness.

Building in Success Factors

A smart trainer builds success factors into the training itself. Following tested procedures and practices, such as conducting a needs assessment and then developing carefully defined learning objectives, automatically builds in key success factors. Following are some other ways you can help to ensure that the training achieves appropriate results.

Evaluation

Results must be evaluated. Can the learner perform as desired after the training is completed? Making sure objectives are clearly measurable is one way to do this. Asking questions (see Step Six) at appropriate times during the session is another. Formulate questions to have on hand to ask at any time. Be sure to have exercises (short, simple ones often suffice) to conduct. Both of these break up the training process, provide continuous feedback, and help keep training focused on objectives.

Motivation

Be conscious of motivation at all times. When you're designing a training segment, for instance, think of ways to generate learner interest (this is critical when the training is to be delivered electronically, without a trainer present). A game or challenge that pits one team against another works well; the challenge often brings out the best in participants and takes advantage of adult learners' desire to increase applicable knowledge. It also keeps the learning process flowing smoothly and energetically. Another highly recommended technique is to have alternatives to move to when you see that learners are losing interest and that what you're doing isn't working. Always bear in mind that your action—and inaction—can greatly influence learner motivation. Stated another way, your passion for your work as a trainer will positively affect learners.

Criteria for Success

Performance-based learning is clearly meaningful to adult learners, and it's the route to successful training. What better built-in feature could there be? Building in evaluation and motivation leads to successful training. It's not enough to focus on performance and to write solid learning objectives that measure desired performance. These objectives, and each learner's achievement of them, must be kept posted for people to see at all times. Thus, feedback becomes one of the most productive ways of building success. If nothing else, add frequent notes in the margins of your trainer's guide (described in Step Four) reminding you to provide feedback. Perhaps a lapel button saying "I love feedback" or a sign taped on the wall saying "Have you provided feedback lately?" would be worth considering.

Conclusion

You've now completed the design phase, although it's virtually impossible to delineate when one part of the training process stops and another begins. Nor does it matter. What does matter is that the right things get done before you actually deliver the training, remembering that the more automated the delivery is to be, the more effort that is required. Now you're ready to build the training.

Step Four

Be Prepared

"As technology continues to permeate nearly every aspect of the business world and as four generations of employees work side by side, delivering the right training in the right way to each group of learners is like performing on the high wire without a net."

—Matt Bolch, *Training*, September 2008

In Step Three we identified training needs. Now it's time to determine how to deliver the training. Getting into the preparation stage, you'll quickly learn a poorly kept trainer's secret: There's never enough time to be fully prepared. The solution: Use your time judiciously—and always bear in mind that the payoff from preparing comes in doing a better job of delivering.

Fully customized classroom training can require as much as one to three days of development for every hour of delivered training. Even off-the-shelf packages require that you put in the time to become familiar with them. Electronically delivered training (via computers and the Internet) can run to hundreds of hours of development time per hour of delivered training. And that's not all. It takes time to prepare to deliver training once it's developed. A rule of thumb given to us by educators is that it takes three hours of preparation time for every one hour of class taught. Of course, electronic learning doesn't have this requirement. The key is to make the most of valuable time in preparing the program. Time is money: It's as simple as that.

Step Four blends the disciplines of training and management. One ingredient is enough technical knowledge to select all the components that compose good training. The other ingredient is the management skill to make intelligent decisions about which components will work best, within a reasonable budget, to get the job done. Guidelines and tools laid out in this critical step of preparing training will help you cut through the technical expertise and decision making you'll need to be prepared for successful training. It would be an easy step if all you needed to do was order a video from a catalog and show it. However, most training requires more than that and demands extensive preparation.

Step Four Summary

Preparation is required in any training situation, whether it's a lengthy customized training program or a brief one that has been used frequently. The reason is that professionalism and performance, together with powerful incentives, combine to keep the trainer working hard to be well prepared. Included within this step are:

- Key principles of preparation
- Selecting delivery methods
- Selecting media
- Selecting evaluation methods
- Selecting facilitators
- Selecting systems for electronically delivered training
- Selecting learners
- Knowing the tools that help decide whether to make or buy
- Knowing the methods for developing experiential exercises
- Using various methods for developing various types of training materials
- Employing tools that help you choose locations and that ensure full preparation

Preparation is a big step, but it is easier if assessment has led to well-defined learning objectives. If the assessment has been done well, the delivery and evaluation steps will be far easier to do. Exhibit 4-1 lists the many activities that may be required to one degree or another if the trainer is to be prepared. As you can see, this step is a big one. It covers a broad spectrum of what trainers do in plying their trade.

Exhibit 4-1. Activities of Step Four: Preparation.

1. *Identification and selection of training materials*
   - Trainer guides
   - Handouts
   - Audiovisual media
   - Specially developed materials
   - Make-or-buy decisions
   - Organizing the flow of the session(s)
   - Timing sessions
   - Experiential exercises
2. *Selection of delivery method*
   - Classroom
   - Self-paced learning
   - Online
   - Audiovisual equipment (e.g., projectors, screens)
   - Computer-based systems
   - Teleconferencing, teletraining
3. *Selection of training participants*
4. *Selection of the training facilitator*
5. *Selection of evaluation methods*
6. *Logistics*
   - Location
   - Arrangement for Internet distribution
   - Arrangement of room and seating
   - Refreshments and meals (as necessary)
   - Travel
   - Participant needs
   - Audiovisual and other equipment
7. *Pilot training*

Key Principles of Preparation

Before delving deeper into this phase, it will be helpful to keep in mind a few key principles while developing training:

1. Proceed as if *you* are going to deliver the training, even if someone else is to do it. There's no surer way to make certain it's complete and will work well. (If this approach doesn't work, approach it as if your boss were going to deliver it.)
2. Keep the eight steps to effective training in mind at all times.
3. Always think in terms of variety (multimodality and multigenerational learners), and implement the concept wherever possible.
4. From time to time, review the adult learning principles outlined in Step Two.
5. Make the training the best you can the first time through; then keep reviewing as time permits to make it better.

Within this step, you'll find examples, lists, and checklists to help you. Start by determining what you need to provide in your training session. If you're making a short presentation where all you have to do is show up and speak, then most of the requirements identified in this step are unnecessary. On the other hand, if you're developing a training session from scratch, one that is to be delivered via the Internet to a large, geographically scattered body of diverse learners, you may find yourself applying most of the information. Examples are used freely with each of the discussions and tools to help you determine the applicability of the elements and prepare for your training.

Making Selections

Training course development can be thought of as a process of making selections about delivery method, media, exercises, learners, and trainers. The first three components must be selected at this time, as should an evaluation method. It's a good idea to select who is to receive the training and who is to deliver it now, as well, because these decisions can affect the final product. Actually, identifying who is to receive training may have been done during needs assessment.

Selecting the Delivery Method

Training has come a long way since the day people first started learning from others. Formalized training has evolved from traditional forms similar to old-fashioned schoolhouse learning (which is still done, particularly in times of economic necessity) to training that is instantly available anywhere, at any time, to any learner with access to the Internet. Suffice it to say that there are more ways to deliver training than you'll likely ever use. The key is to choose the one that works well, which means within your means and time frame.

Types of Delivery Methods

In actual practice, many of the ways to deliver training can be combined, the blend providing perhaps the most effective approach. For our discussion, three primary categories have been selected: classroom, self-paced, and media driven (recognizing that there is overlap and blending of the types). Among them, the delivery methods you might find useful can be identified.

Classroom

This category is a traditional one and is a commonly used method of training delivery. It's effective, and most organizations have suitable rooms in which to hold training classes (if not, commercial spaces are readily available). One of the main reasons this method is still used is that it's comfortable, it's the way most of us have conducted training, and it has a lot of things going for it, including cost—it's less expensive to develop and usually takes less time to deliver than some other methods. When we think of training, in fact, older learners may immediately picture an instructor standing on a platform in front of the room, marker in hand, projector nearby, and students paying attention as training is presented. Actually, this is only part of the process of classroom training. It can also encompass some of the following activities:

- *Lecture*, with the instructor presenting detailed information—for example, the company accounting manager conducting a class on a new tax requirement that requires new travel record keeping. (Make this as interactive as possible to avoid potential boredom.)

- *Demonstration,* with someone demonstrating the proper way to do something for the attendees to observe and learn—for example, a technician showing administrative staff how to make computer system backups with a new type of handheld storage device.
- *Discussion,* as the total training effort or part of an overall training program (see Step Six). Because of how adults learn, discussion should be a natural part of all training (including online).
- *Seminars,* with pertinent topics discussed by learners, possibly in small groups, in order to attain maximum participation of all in attendance. This could range from discussing a lengthy case study to a short newspaper article related to the topic at hand.
- *Exercises,* usually done in small groups to maximize participation. For a class on workplace safety, exercises can range from simple events (e.g., having learners work in pairs to fill out an accident report) to major events (e.g., having learners lay out and walk through a complete accident investigation).
- *Laboratory sessions,* exercises associated with systems and equipment. Most computer-related training falls into this category. The lab sessions are essential for learning how to use the system or equipment. For example, training on any type of software package would require hands-on lab time, as would training on how to use telecommunications systems.

Self-Paced

Self-paced training has the potential to be extremely valuable because it can be conducted at times convenient to the learner—commuting to work, whiling away time when television fare is unexciting, or during the morning jog or walk. It works well when learners are at remote locations, when the training isn't conducted often, and when there's motivation to learn on one's own. Of prime concern to the trainer is that it allows learning to take place without a facilitator. For persons eager to learn, this could mean a considerable amount of learning going on outside the workplace.

There are a number of ways to deliver self-paced training, ranging from simple paper-and-pencil assignments to sophisticated media approaches:

- *Workbooks.* This can be a combination of textual material and exercises and questions for the reader to complete at intervals.

Programmed learning texts, where learners follow instructions and progress according to whether they have answered questions correctly, fit this category. The purpose is to guide the learner through material needed to achieve desired objectives. Usually these media are designed so that learners achieve success 90 percent of the time, keeping learning on a positive basis. Instead of a workbook, you can distribute a checklist to be completed while the trainee is learning on the job; a supervisor initials items that have been demonstrated. This is also called on-the-job training and is more than just turning people loose to learn on their own.

- *Mentoring and Coaching.* Assigning qualified staff members as mentor or coach of a learner is a widely used form of self-paced learning. A *mentor* gives advice on career moves and workplace-related situations. A *coach* helps the learner through skills learning, possibly using checklists or workbooks, as well as demonstrating skills and critiquing the trainee's performance.

- *Audio.* Audio learning has been around for quite a while, but technology has added a new twist—podcasts—that makes them more portable and usable on demand than ever. Audio programs are downloaded from the source, such as corporate headquarters, to individual computers or handheld devices. Learners can then listen to them while sitting at their workstations or using their portable players. This is a great way to supplement other training, reinforce learning, and provide audio learners with means of learning new materials. A wide variety of topics can be made available to learners.

- *Visual Media.* This includes DVD and videotape as a primary training medium. Visual media can cover a wide range of standard topics where training is required (e.g., customer relations, sexual harassment, sales, leadership). They can add a greater dimension to training because they can include learning-specific segments that can include graphics, video, and sound. As with podcasts, video programs can be downloaded by learners for viewing at their workstations or on portable devices. Note: If you have videotapes rather than a DVD, make sure the player you will use can play them.

Media-Driven

More and more training programs are delivered by technological means. Media-driven programs are highly interesting to learners, and they take advantage of the latest technology—but they are expensive. Another characteristic is that there are plenty of combinations to choose from, as you'll see from the following descriptions. One of the significant developments in personal computing is that multimedia presentations (CD, DVD, sound, video) can be fully exploited through computer-driven training. (A word of caution: There are as many terms as there are people who have been involved in the evolution of computers applied to training.) Here are some choices:

- *Computer-Based Training.* A computer controls all the functions. One way computers are frequently used to deliver training is through implementation of a configuration specifically for training: the personal computer (PC) presents programs that contain training segments. The program, similar to an application program, is made to deliver training. Maintenance activities lend themselves well to this form, as does any subject where graphics are necessary. Computer-based training offers alphanumeric, graphics, animation, sound, and full-motion video capabilities. The learner interacts by answering queries presented by the program, perhaps by touching the screen, and solving problems presented by the computer training program. (See the section on use of the Internet to deliver training, where the course material is accessible on a Web site rather than on a DVD.)
- *Simulation.* This has been used for some time by the military and aviation industry to train pilots. Highly realistic flight simulators, with full-motion cockpits and actual cockpit controls, have taught thousands of pilots to land on aircraft carriers, handle emergency situations, and in general learn to fly aircraft they've never set foot in. Simulations for the workplace continue to grow in number. Realistic workplace situations can be mirrored using simulation, which can be used for management development and leadership training. Emergency response teams can be trained in realistic environments. This is an area that will likely continue to expand.

- *Teleconferencing.* This can refer to anything from a conference call, where a small group of individuals are conducting a seminar, to a worldwide hookup via satellite, where several hundred people are online at the same time, fully visible to one another and able to interact as if they were in the same room. The options selected—audio, video, or computer based—depend on need and availability. Teleconferencing has these advantages:
  —Brings a large number of participants together at the same time
  —Can be completely interactive, much the same as if everyone were in the same room
  —Eliminates expensive travel and related costs
  —Takes less time away from workplace
  —Can reach remote locations
  —Can get urgent topics online quickly
  —Can incorporate text messaging so that participants can communicate directly with one another

By blending various methods to meet your needs, you can obtain a number of advantages: rapid delivery, ease of preparation, and a lively format, for example. For instance, you might use a commercially available DVD for initial training to meet fast turnaround demand, while developing your own workbooks and DVD for ongoing training.

Internet

Much of what has been said about computer-based training also applies to the Internet, which is the repository for training programs that learners can access training anytime, anywhere they may be (as long as they have an Internet connection). The difference is that the learner goes to the training Web site, signs in, and starts training—and learning. It's convenient, reaches virtually any employee, anywhere, and is available whenever the employee has time to train. It is completely interactive and can include sophisticated graphics, simulations, and more. There is no need for instructors, but someone will have to evaluate the recorded results. Virtually any subject that can be taught in a classroom can be automated and made available to the learner via the Internet.

A note on developing online materials: For best results, constantly put yourself in the learner's place and visualize how effective the online delivered course will be. Remember, all the principles of learning apply; it's just that you will not be on hand to make sure the learner gets by the rough spots. Use of e-mail, blog sites, and text messaging can keep you connected with all learners, although having a responsible person available for feedback is highly beneficial (i.e., a trainer who can quickly respond to learners).

Selection Criteria

Great care must be taken when selecting media to ensure a positive return on investment. In times when every dollar spent must be fully accounted for, it's imperative for the trainer to make bottom-line-related decisions. Factors to consider in selecting delivery methods are cost, ease of modifying, and degree of use.

Cost

A number of factors are related to cost, starting with possibly the biggest consideration: your budget. Unless you've had plenty of lead time to factor in cost elements, the budget often sets the level of spending before you embark on your training endeavor. Obviously you can't spend more than has been allotted, unless special circumstances arise.

The next thing to consider, and the most important in the long run, is whether you can justify the expense on the basis of a return on investment (ROI) calculation. This is just another business decision, the same as buying capital equipment, acquiring facilities, and purchasing raw materials and supplies. There must be a return on investment to justify an expenditure. This is made easier if you've been thorough in determining how much you believe performance, productivity, or other critical measurements will be improved through training. You must be able to show how faster processing turnaround times will reduce costs and more than pay for training or be able to show how reducing stress, which you can do through training, will result in fewer sick days, fewer errors, lower medical costs, and so on.

If new resources are required, a prime consideration is whether they're reusable. If you decided that e-learning is justified, you must consider to what use the systems will be put after training is completed. If the training will be ongoing or the systems can be used for multiple purposes, the expenditure becomes easier to justify.

Another consideration is the applicability of the delivery system to your requirements. If the staff being trained uses computers for a major portion of their job execution, does it make sense to give them a training package that uses paper and pencil? If they're accustomed to working on their own, does it make sense to use anything other than a self-paced approach? Related to these considerations is whether the equipment and resources are already available. If PCs already sit on everyone's desk, it makes sense to consider using them for training. If facilities for recording and updating CDs are in place, then consider using them for training. If technology and resources are available (e.g., operational systems like computers and networks), then these move to the top of the list of possible delivery methods. And, finally, will you be able to use the equipment for other training? If so, then you have added reasons to seriously consider using a particular delivery system. (A word of caution: In bad economic times, cost cutting becomes the first order of business—and training is one of the first, if not the first, areas of business to be cut back. What this means is that no matter how successful e-learning might have been, for instance, funding cuts will nevertheless cause training to revert to less expensive classroom delivery.)

Ease of Modification

How often will training require modification? It's one thing to issue change pages to written material, particularly when it can be sent to remote sites electronically. It's quite another to update training programs that have been recorded on media, or posted on a Web site. If it's to be a highly used training program, modification costs can be justified on that basis.

Degree of Usage

Four quantitative considerations need to be made for this selection factor:

American Management Association
www.amanet.org

1. How many people are to be trained—the more there are, the easier it is to justify e-learning
2. How geographically dispersed they are—travel costs are a definite consideration
3. How often the training will be conducted—the more often the training, the more justifiable e-learning or computer-based training
4. How long the training program is to be in use—the longer the term, the more sensible it is to automate it

Rules of Thumb

Exhibit 4-2 summarizes the factors to consider when choosing delivery method. In addition, here are a few general rules to follow when making a decision:

- Remember that classroom training is the quickest and the easiest to develop (the reason it becomes more popular in tough economic times and is popular in good times, as well).
- Use existing equipment whenever possible (including word processing, reproduction, graphics, and visual equipment).
- For training on using equipment and systems, practice on the actual systems as training devices whenever possible.
- Get help when using high-technology approaches (e.g., computer-based training, e-learning, teleconferencing).
- Think multimodality when choosing what to do, and use as many different methods as possible (and cost effective), remembering that simple variations work well, too.

If you need more analysis and information to make a decision, consult your training department or a qualified outside provider.

Selecting Media

Selecting media runs hand-in-hand with selecting delivery method since media have become primary delivery methods. Certainly, the distinction between media and delivery methods has become blurred. Computer-based training is a case in point. It can be either a medium used in the classroom or a primary (possibly stand-alone) method of delivering.

Exhibit 4-2. Selecting delivery methods and media.

Type	Use and Selection Factors
Classroom	• Best for knowledge-based learning
	• Good when you need to work in groups
	• Good when you need to train in a hurry
	• Requires little follow-on
	• Requires frequent updating
	• Technology can easily be brought in
	• Video can be used easily
	• Interactivity is easy to facilitate
Self-paced	• Useful when learners are widely separated geographically
	• Good when on-the-job training is the primary method of delivering training
	• Good when multimodality isn't critical
	• Enables supervisors to coach and track progress
	• Any technology required has built-in step
	• Useful when there are large numbers of learners or when learners are geographically separated
	• Good when there is an ongoing requirement for repeated training
Media-driven	• Requires that necessary equipment, systems, and software be available
	• Good when there is a heavy use of technology in the workplace
	• Technology and training systems readily available

Types of Media

For this discussion, media are divided into the general categories of *basic*—what has traditionally been used and is likely to be readily available (e.g., classroom and written media)—and *advanced*, which is associated more with technology (e.g., virtual reality and expert systems) and generally requires more expertise to develop materials and use for training.

Basic Media

This category includes everything we usually think about when the words *education* and *training* arise, because they're generally associated with classroom usage. All these media are extensively used. Even though training relies heavily on being wired (or wireless as the case might be) and digitized, the old-fashioned tools of whiteboards and projectors continue to serve, and serve well. Tips on how to use media are found in Step Five and will be helpful as you make decisions about which basic media to choose, as ease of use is a prime reason for selection. Some media, such as video, fall into both the basic and the advanced categories. Following are the media classified under this category:

- *Dry Boards and Chalkboards.* They're almost always available and require no technical expertise other than that you be able to write (legibly, we hope).
- *Flip Charts.* Readily available and portable, they offer many advantages, particularly for capturing participant thoughts for later review, update, and application.
- *Overhead Projectors.* They're inexpensive and portable, and it's easy to make transparencies (all you need is a copy machine or laser printer). Color adds to the value of visual aids, and the graphics and word-processing capabilities of PCs make graphics and color for transparencies readily available.
- *Off-the-Shelf Video.* Monitors and DVD/VCR players are plentiful, and there are literally thousands of videos available on a vast array of topics.
- *Audio.* This requires computers and portable devices that enable the use of podcasts. Off-the-shelf topics are plentiful, and it's easy to generate custom audio quickly if the proper system is installed.

Advanced Media

Thanks to technology, you have many choices of media to use in delivering training. Most of these are directly related to the PC and to the powerful peripherals associated with them. Following are the ones to consider when developing training:

- *Video.* Video can be customized for your use (e.g., to demonstrate a technique covered in the training or to deliver a motivational message to learners). You must have the proper equipment and the expertise to develop the videos, although small, stabilized camcorders work quite well. Regular training sessions can be filmed, but best results come from carefully rehearsed and staged presentations. Videos can also be embedded into computer-delivered training, including online. Note: Videos have replaced film, and many former training films (e.g., 16mm) have been converted to DVD.
- *Projection Methods.* This includes the ability to make hard copy from handwritten material on special boards and systems that can produce a variety of media through computers (digital presentations, slides, posters, charts, transparencies). Media service bureaus can produce the projected media from programs.
- *Computer-Based Training.* This requires authoring system software, appropriate hardware (including peripheral media such as CD-ROMs), and a qualified person to develop the lessons. It can take advantage of color, graphics, and a host of other technology that improves the learning process.
- *Internet.* Training can be uploaded to a Web site that is accessible to learners and can include many types of media.
- *Interactive Video.* This requires all the media already discussed plus multimedia equipment that offers a wide array of capabilities.
- *Presentation Software.* These systems for making computer-generated presentations for output to various devices and media, as well as allowing information to be projected directly from the computer onto a large screen, take full advantage of presentation system capabilities to produce powerful programs. These systems lend themselves to a wide variety of training needs. Note: 35mm slides, long a training media staple, have been converted to digital where appropriate. Software packages are available that convert presentations and incorporate them into training packages.
- *Digital Projectors.* These are used to project computer images onto a screen. The combination of a laptop computer and a digital projector makes a highly portable training presentation system.
- *Liquid Crystal Displays.* These projection devices fit onto an overhead projector and project images from computer to a large screen. Large-screen video displays and projectors can also be used.
- *Simulators.* These can be specially built; they are expensive. PCs have made great strides here because of powerful simulation

software that can emulate other systems. Simulation generated by virtual reality is the most advanced form.

- *Expert Systems.* These programs capture human decision-making and diagnosis methods and are made available to end users to assist in a variety of functions and professions. Such programs can easily be added to training sessions.

Selection Criteria

Criteria for selecting media are closely related to those for selecting delivery methods. This has become even more the case as training and education have adopted the concept of using multimodality to deliver training that appeals to all learning styles. The ultimate concern is to deliver the most effective training, taking into consideration return on training investment.

Make-or-Buy Decisions

No question about it—it's cheaper to buy ready-made training than to develop training from scratch. Custom-made training is for organizations that can afford it—but there's a catch. Organizations are different from one another, as are the people in them. Needs arise that are unique, and off-the-shelf training programs don't always meet those needs. The result is that it may become necessary to initiate a make-or-buy decision-making process. The bottom-line secret is still quite simple: Does the training achieve the performance objectives you need to meet?

We have a number of choices when it comes to procuring training:

1. *Develop in-house from scratch*—if you have staff, time, and other resources available or can contract out the work.
2. *Purchase complete packages from vendors*—if the packages fulfill most of your needs.
3. *Send learners off to let someone else do the training*—if you have the time and resources to do this and the other person's training fills the bill.
4. *Modify or adapt existing packages*—if you have the staff, time, and resources and if the training comes reasonably close to being what you need.

Other combinations could be developed, but these take care of most situations. A word of advice—even if designing a training program from scratch, it is good practice to first research what is available, if only to get ideas on how to design and build your training package.

Several factors can help you determine whether to make or buy training, starting with the budget:

1. *Budget.* Even if there is justification for making large expenditures, if the funds aren't available, then developing a unique, customized program may be out of the question. Cash flow is always a consideration.
2. *Criticality of Training.* If company performance against growing competition is at issue, then spending the money to get the best training available is probably justified.
3. *Number of People to be Trained.* If just a few employees are to be trained, it may be more sensible to send them away; if it's hundreds, customizing may be well worth the effort.
4. *Frequency of Training.* How often will training be conducted? If not often, then find the best that is commercially available.
5. *Location of Training.* Will you use multiple locations or only the home office? For multiple locations, geographic separation can be a central factor in designing training.
6. *Applicability of Off-the-Shelf Materials.* The materials need to be mostly, if not 100 percent, applicable (although it may be cost effective to use only that which is applicable and ignore the rest).
7. *Need for Customizing.* How close does the material come to filling your need? To what extent must it be altered?
8. *Format.* Do the format and delivery method fit your need? For example, if the available training is on video, do you have VHS players or only DVD players and monitors available?
9. *Availability of Trainers.* You need both qualified instructors and developers.
10. *Availability of Resources* (computers, equipment, space, material).

Some of these factors will be more important to you than others. Weigh the factors on the basis of your needs and the available resources to help you see if one method stands out from the others (see Exhibit 4-3). You can select the key factors and assign values to them, then develop a decision matrix. In evaluating a particular training package, values ranging from 1 to 10 can be assigned to such factors as cost, number of people to be trained, frequency, applicability, format, and availability of trainers qualified to use the package. In this example, the highest value possible is 50. You may determine that a value as high as 40 will make the package a viable choice. Use of online training will likely result in a highly weighted score.

Exhibit 4-3. Sample weighting factors for making selection decisions.

Factor	High-Degree/ Weight	Low-Degree/ Weight
• Criticality of training	• Urgent	• Not urgent
• Number of participants	• Large	• Small
• Frequency of delivering	• Often	• Once or infrequently
• Location of learners	• Many locations	• All or most at home office
• Training materials	• Must be customized	• Available off-the-shelf

Selecting and Developing Experiential Exercise

Interaction is one of the secrets to success in training. Learning theory, new and old, and brain-related research on what makes people successful add to our knowledge of how best to interact. Interaction can be between the learner and subject material or equipment (e.g., via the Internet), between the facilitator and learners (e.g., in the classroom), and between learners (e.g., text messaging). "All the above" is the best way. Any way interaction involving learners can be stimulated will help you succeed as a training facilitator. In short, experiential exercises are perhaps the best way people learn. (This concept is expanded in Step Five.)

Varieties of Exercises

There are many exercises to use with learners. Here are some common ones:

- *Icebreakers,* to get training sessions off to a good start. They can range from something as simple as having people introduce themselves, perhaps having them answer a specific question about themselves, all the way to definitive exercises, such as bingo games and puzzle solving. (You'll find some samples in Step Six.)

- *Climate setting,* to get into the subject early on. These are topic specific. For example, if the session is to be on listening skills, the exercise could be one that demonstrates how difficult it is to be a good listener.

- *Perception,* because this concept affects much of what we do and who we are. Perception exercises do an excellent job of illustrating the concept of multiple, and sometimes contradictory, viewpoints. These often require a visual aid, perhaps one with figures that can be interpreted in more than one way.

- *Team building,* to get teams up and running. These exercises are popular because learners usually enjoy participating. Often learners are broken into small groups and given problems to solve or tasks to perform. These exercises are designed to promote teamwork and illustrate the importance of teams. They might also combine other subject matter, such as group communication or problem-solving skills.

- *Problem solving,* to help develop this important skill. This can be used for team building or to have learners solve problems using a specific problem-solving method they're learning. Or it could be an exercise to solve a particular type of problem, such as determining return on investment for a management training course.

- *Leadership,* possibly designed to show how the absence of leadership leads to problems or to demonstrate specific leadership traits.

- *Determining roles,* to help people determine what their roles are. This could be part of team building, where the task is for learners to choose which role they want in a given exercise situation, which directly parallels what happens in real life.

- *Self-concepts,* which lie at the bottom of skills acquisition. These are designed to help determine what people's views

are on certain issues, such as prejudice for a diversity training session. These might also be part of personality- or
leadership-related exercises or intended to help participants
determine their learning styles.

These are representative of how exercises are used in training
settings, and there are many others. As you can see, some are closely
related, and it's easy to add to the list.

Forms of Exercises

Exercises come in many forms, from the exchange of a few words,
to paper-and-pencil challenges, to reviews of corporate cases using
advanced computer technology. The ones described here provide a
widely varied set from which to choose. Keep in mind that using a
variety of exercise types usually contributes positively to training.
Remember also that, for classroom training, exercises break up presentations and keep learners on their toes and motivated. Here are
some of the more commonly used types:

1. *Instruments.* Often used to identify personality or learning traits
   or to measure attitudes and climates (as noted in Step Two regarding needs assessment), they can be for individual or group
   use. Examples of instruments for individual determinations include those to identify personal needs and motivational traits
   (e.g., participant, power, or affiliation orientation), teaching
   styles, learning styles, or personality types. Group-related instruments are used to determine group perceptions of management practices, readiness to change, and so forth. It's important
   that the correct instrument be selected (readymade, customized,
   or combination) and that the facilitator be thoroughly familiar
   with it. Some instruments (e.g., Myers Briggs) require qualified
   individuals to be able to use them properly.
2. *Case Studies.* Similar to the ones used in business schools, they
   have achieved wide use as training tools, largely because they
   represent the actual business world. They can be procured off
   the shelf or be custom made for specific training situations and
   organizations. In fact, the case presented may well be a current management challenge that must be resolved. Numerous

cases can be found daily in the business news. Case studies are equally useful to nonprofit organizations.

3. *Role Plays.* Adding to the reality of behavioral training (e.g., diversity, customer relations), role plays have long been used in marketing and sales training. Role plays require some expertise to facilitate, and not all learners are comfortable with them. However, they can be the next best thing to actual situations. There's much to be gained when a participant can feel the pain of the representative on the other end of an irate customer's tirade or of someone who has just been discriminated against.

4. *Games.* These can be manual or automated, simple or quite involved. An example of a simple game is one in which participants are placed in a hypothetical situation of having been shipwrecked and must choose from a list of items those that they believe would help them survive. More complex games can be computer based and may involve giant corporations that must make a variety of financial, legal, and other management decisions in a highly competitive environment. Good games can get learners heavily involved in the learning process (and younger learners will be right at home with games), while taking advantage of one of the keys to adult learning.

5. *Simulations.* These usually bring to mind flight simulators, but simulations are used in other areas. For example, there are sophisticated computer games that simulate highly articulated business situations. Games and simulations are closely related.

6. *Group Discussion and Seminars.* These may involve a simple exercise of presenting small groups with readings and then having the groups discuss them, possibly answering a predetermined set of questions. Variations may involve having one group represent management and another labor or perhaps the governmental and competitive interests. The key is to get the learners involved in the subject matter and issues presented in the material. Debates on key issues within the training context provide a challenging option that can get participants fully and enthusiastically involved.

7. *Practical Work.* This format imitates actual work situations in which learners must perform. Computer training lends itself to this format, as does learning any type of equipment or system.

Learners can prepare a purchase order using the new system that was the subject of the training session, for example.

8. *Demonstrations.* This can be useful for complex situations or for ones where there are not enough systems for everyone to have one. For example, a training session on how to program and use a new assembly-line robot might start with a demonstration by an expert user. Learners can then take turns on the available equipment. Behavioral training also fits well, since both proper and improper behaviors (e.g., in dealing with customers) can be demonstrated. Computer-related demonstrations can be projected using media.

9. *Outdoor Programs.* These include survival situations and fitness, where learners become completely involved while acquiring teamwork, problem-solving, and creativity skills. These programs usually require some physical prowess, ranging anywhere from desert survival for pilots to tugs-of-war for team members.

10. *Assessment Centers.* These are settings in which actual work situations are set up and participants must deal with them. For example, in-basket or e-mail file exercises in which participants must make decisions based on action items in their files are often used with new management trainees, who must make decisions about how to set priorities.

Instruments, case studies, games, simulation, group discussion (e.g., through chat rooms), practical work, and demonstrations (e.g., through embedded videos) can all be incorporated into computer-based and Internet-delivered training.

When to Use Exercises

Exercises can be used at virtually any time during a training session for a wide variety of purposes. These include:

- *Getting Everyone Started on the Right Track and Acquainted with One Another.* It's one sure way for learners to become involved from the beginning.
- *Team Building.* Given the importance of teams to the workplace, this training ranks among the top in terms of need.

- *Introducing New Material.* This takes the mystery out of learning, particularly when people must learn something they have never been faced with before. First-time computer users fare much better when they get their feet wet at the outset of training, and the way to do it is to sit them down at the computer.
- *Reinforcing Material Presented during a Training Session.*
- *Providing a Multimodality Approach* (particularly if the training is of the classroom type, stressing lecture presentation). Exercises are relatively easy ways to add variety.
- *Illustrating Actual Situations.* This is important in a work environment where lack of knowledge about how to deal with specific situations and lack of skills to deal with them can be costly. Let the mistakes be made—and learning take place—through exercises in the training setting.
- *Demonstrating How Things Work.* This is especially helpful when the things in question are complex.
- *Modeling Behavior*—both the right and the wrong approaches.
- *Measuring Performance or Progress.* For performance-based learning, an exercise is a much better test of whether a learning objective has been achieved to a satisfactory level than a paper-and-pencil test.
- *Measuring Current Skills and Knowledge.* This is similar to measuring learning objectives, except that it may be done before the training as well.

Key Considerations for Exercise Selection

Keep these key considerations in mind when selecting or developing exercises:

- Be creative.
- Use what is available as much as possible.
- Use short exercises during training to break up material.
- Remember that variety is the spice of life.
- Keep the exercises as realistic as possible. This is what adults prefer.

Resources for Exercises

Fortunately, there are plenty of resources available. Because exercises and games are so widely used, numerous books and online materials are on the market, available from a variety of sources (see Steps Five and Eight and the appendix on Resources for the First-Time Trainer for further discussion).

Selecting Evaluation Methods

The reason for selecting the evaluation method at this time is to make sure it's tied into the learning objectives. Also, this decision can be made more easily at this point in the process, and it may be necessary to develop tests or evaluation exercises, which need to be prepared in advance.

The necessary balance for evaluating training is that the method used be as simple as possible while ensuring that training results are measured. The more formal the training, the greater the possible need for highly developed evaluation methods.

There are three primary evaluation methods: verbal, written, and performance tests (e.g., to demonstrate that the learner can generate a spreadsheet, operate the piece of machinery, or use the desired technique for dealing with customer queries). Step Seven, Get Feedback, includes detailed information on this.

Selecting Participants

With few exceptions, resources (i.e., money and staff) for training are limited, so the key is to make sure the people being trained absolutely need it. If a person doesn't need a particular training course (if, for example, it's a supervisory management session and a person isn't due to be promoted for several months), then don't include that person; newly acquired skills that aren't applied right away are soon forgotten. Training should be performance based, so participants should be the ones who will perform the skills in question. Here are some selection criteria to use when determining who should attend training:

- Learners who were identified during needs analysis
- Learners for whom the training is directly pertinent to the person's job

- Learners who will be able to use the skills soon after they return to work
- Learners who meet prerequisites and need the skills
- Learners who are almost certain to be able to achieve the learning objectives (If they can't, preliminary or remedial training may be justified. Training can be designed and used to screen people, but it's the exception.)
- Learners for whom funding is available
- Learners whose time away from work can be cost justified
- Learners whose increased productivity after training will considerably outweigh the lost work time caused by their absence (This consideration is greatly reduced for Internet-based training.)
- Learners who are motivated to participate

When necessary and appropriate, prioritize who should attend classroom training. Keep a waiting list in case primary attendees cancel at the last moment.

Selecting Facilitators

As the workplace becomes more complex, so does training. For this reason, training facilitators often are subject matter experts. The challenge is to find facilitators—trainers—who are both expert in the subject and good trainers. Perhaps this is the reason you were chosen, so the eight steps described in this book will lead you to become a successful facilitator. Whatever the situation, it's imperative that both elements—subject matter expertise and facilitation skills—be present in the chosen facilitator. As a summary, here are the considerations, in addition to subject matter expertise and facilitation skills, when selecting the person to be facilitator:

- Availability
- The trade-off between preparation time and lost productivity (will the lost productivity of the expert be offset by his or her contribution to the training effort?)
- Previous experience
- How many of the eight steps must be accomplished (e.g., is it only for delivering the training that a person is being chosen?)

- Funding (e.g., if needs dictate that an outsider be brought in, are there funds to pay the person?)
- Skills (e.g., does the person have them?)
- Credibility (e.g., will learners accept the person as expert?)
- Motivation (e.g., will the facilitator be motivated and motivate learners?)

Organizing Training

Organizing training lessons or modules is a process of sequencing learning events. Most training is job and performance oriented, meaning it follows a logical sequence of events. Organizing training into workable modules starts with the learning objectives. The terms *lesson* and *module* are often used interchangeably by trainers. For a large-scale training course, you may need to form modules that, in turn, have a certain number of lessons in them, but, for our purposes, the discussion will be kept simple.

Modularity is a vital consideration when training materials become a finished product ready for delivery. Keep the result as modular as possible, for two reasons. One is that doing so follows the logical process of laying out training. The training itself will most likely fall into modules—groupings of materials and learning objectives that make sense. The other reason is that it makes the training more amenable to updating; you can simply pull out the modules that need a change, make them, and put the package back together again. Modularity also allows training to commence as soon as an individual module is completed, rather than making the training wait until the entire course is finalized.

How to Sequence

When subject matter is presented—a political speech, college lecture, sermon, planning report, or major training session—it must be presented in an orderly, logical manner if it is to make sense to the recipient. This means the presenter must have properly organized it in the first place. Fortunately, this isn't difficult to do. Exhibit 4-4 lays out a process to help you make sure training sessions are logical and orderly—and successfully presented. Make sure the learning objectives can be achieved in the time you estimate you need to complete a session.

Exhibit 4-4. How to organize a training session.

1. *Start with learning objectives.*
   - Organize objectives into a logical sequence of lessons.
   - From this sequence, form groups of lessons to create a preliminary set of training modules. Note: Some training courses may consist of only one module, while others may comprise several modules covering several hours or days of training.
   - Use these groupings to form the final modules, or lessons, of your training.
   - Don't have too many objectives in one lesson (e.g., six objectives in a one-hour presentation or online lesson, with an exercise, is probably too many).

2. *Analyze and sort each grouping of objectives.*
   - Form the objectives into a lesson.
   - Treat each objective as a major element of the lesson.
   - Put the objectives of each module into logical order. (You may decide to move a few objectives around later, so this can still be a preliminary module.)
   - Identify elements to be included with each objective. These are the learning elements that may be needed to address the objective (e.g., an objective to parallel-park a car might include elements of backing up, using rearview mirrors, and improving spatial judgment).

3. *Organize the lesson.*
   - Sequence the objectives and elements into the order you want them.
   - Add detail as necessary for the presentation.

4. *Determine times.*
   - Determine the approximate time it will take to present each objective.
   - Add up times to determine the length of the module.

5. *Review the lesson, making any adjustments necessary.*

6. *Follow this process for each remaining grouping of objectives.*

Another way to think of this is to view it as *chunking*, which means just what it says: breaking the material into chunks. Each chunk should make sense, though it doesn't have to stand alone. Suppose the topic is how to overcome prospective customers' objections to purchasing a maintenance contract when buying a new copy machine. The chunks might be:

- A review of standard options for maintenance, including payment methods
- A list of reasons that maintenance contracts save the customer money over the long haul
- A list of potential customer objections
- A step-by-step process of how to deal with each objection
- A method for asking for the order once objections are overcome

There's nothing scientific about chunking. In fact, it's the way many people learn. They absorb one chunk at a time until they have learned the whole lesson or skill. Using the developed learning objectives and common sense, particularly when the session is of a technical, subject matter orientation, will ensure that your training flows smoothly.

Storyboarding

Another approach is to *storyboard* the module, that is, to identify the most important elements of the module (learning objectives) and present the message accordingly. This is the process media people use to develop television commercials. When you think how hard-hitting and attention-getting an ad must be, you can see how applicable this format could be to developing training. There are software packages available to assist in developing your storyboard.

Here are the steps to follow for storyboarding (a sample storyboard worksheet is shown in Exhibit 4-5):

1. Identify the key elements (objectives) of the module. Each of these becomes a frame.
2. At the top of a separate sheet of paper, write the frame number, subject, and learning objective or theme sentence.
3. Organize the elements into a logical sequence, adjusting frame numbers as appropriate.

Exhibit 4-5. Sample storyboard worksheet.

Frame No.:_____ Lesson/Presentation Title:_____ Date:_____

Subject/Learning Objective of This Frame: _____ Identify speaker concerns.

Theme Sentence/Learning Objective: Success in being a good listener starts with being able to determine why the

speaker needs to be listened to.

Amplifying Information	Illustration/Action/Reference
Reasons to be heard	Video showing failure of supervisor to pick up on a subordinate's concern
• Personal problem	Discussion group
• Workplace-related problem	
• Lack of knowledge about a	
work matter	Brainstorm session to identify reasons that people need to be listened to
• Simply lonely	
• Concerns about goals and	
objectives	Brainstorm to identify ways to find out what is causing the problem

Time required to complete: 20 minutes

4. Add subtopics to each key element to amplify the information.
5. Organize the subtopics into a logical sequence by numbering them in desired order.
6. Add visuals and exercises to the storyboard (these go on the right side). Also include references, related stories, or anything else that will illustrate the frame.
7. Add times to each element to compute the estimated time for each module.

Using a Trainer's Guide

The sequencing process creates the input for the outline section of the trainer's guide. Even if key information is written down on the back of an envelope for a hastily put-together management presentation, some representation of the guide is a must. (The exception is if the trainer has a photographic mind.) Keeping these online and available to those who might need them (including learners who can learn a lot simply by reviewing them) will make this and all other materials more valuable to everyone. Exhibit 4-6 shows the contents of a trainer's guide. Possibly the only difference between a trainer's guide and a learner's guide is that the trainer's might have test answers in it.

Other Materials

Trainers use a wide variety of materials, many of them in paper form, to present training. This is despite significant efforts on the part of organizations to become more environmentally friendly, or green. The ability to quickly generate training materials is facilitated by readily available office machines. These materials can also be presented digitally for computer-based and Internet training.

Handouts

Handouts can range from a single piece of paper summarizing the entire training session (usually the approach taken for busy executives who attend training and briefing sessions) to an outline for learners to fill in as the session progresses, perhaps in a thick notebook. In between these extremes, there are charts, books,

Exhibit 4-6. Trainer's guide contents.

Part One: General Information

- Title of course/module and other pertinent information
- Date of latest revision and responsible person
- Learning objectives
- Target audience
- Prerequisites and learner participation
- Learner materials (e.g., handouts, exercises)
- Instructor materials
- Audiovisual requirements
- Room setup requirements
- References
- Length of session/module

Part Two: The Session

Estimated time for each major segment	Topic/event	Activity, visual, and handout
	• Main topics in outline form	
	• Introduction to session:	
	—Introductions/icebreakers	
	—Topics to be covered	
	• First major topic (learning objective):	
	As much detail in outline as needed to ensure that facilitator thoroughly covers material	
	• Second major topic	
	• Additional major topics	
	• Summary	
	Questions	
	Evaluation	
	Preparation for next session	

For a session on listening skills, the guide might look like this:

Time	Topic/event	Activity, visual, and handout
5 min.	Introduction of participants • Discuss reasons for answers • Review what is to be covered	Think of a person you know who is not a good listener
10 min.	Why listening is important • From supervisor's viewpoint • From workers' viewpoint • From management viewpoint	• Visual 1 • Visual 2 • Visual 3 • Visual 4
10 min.	Good listening techniques	• Video depicting how to listen
10 min.	Detail the step used in video • Discuss with learners	• Visual 5
20 min.	Exercise to demonstrate good skills • Divide into groups and give instructions	Exercise, using handouts
10 min.	Wrap-up and review of exercise	

actual work material—in fact, anything that augments the learning process. A word of caution: Do not overload the learners with too much information—and be conscious of efforts to make the workplace greener. This is where electronics, which enable the learner to access information randomly without carrying around an armload of materials, comes in handy.

The advantage of a complete handout is that learners can concentrate on the task of learning, particularly if the subject is highly technical. On the other hand, you can use outlines to be filled in when there is a great deal of knowledge learning involved—for example, when employees are being trained to implement a new quality control program. The outline can include major topics, and the learner is asked to take note of key points as the session progresses. The combination of paying close attention to the presentation and taking notes can contribute to the learning process, particularly when there's an exercise or other activity to reinforce the material.

Another type of handout is useful for sessions where visual aids play a large role. Providing copies of the visuals (e.g., a computer-generated graphic presentation) helps participants follow the presentation while making notes on the handout, which usually helps them more readily recall them later. Thanks to electronic systems, many handouts can be distributed digitally and save a lot of paper.

Visual Aids

Visual aids, like handouts, must be prepared in advance. These are specialized materials to be used on the media selected. (See the discussion in Step Five on how to use media.) The key point to remember is that these must be designed and produced with all the other materials. Computer graphic programs make visual generation, whether for a chart to be hung on the wall or a full-blown presentation, quite easy.

Miscellaneous Materials

As with most other subjects, training has its miscellaneous materials category. This is needed because just about anything can be classified as a training aid as long as it contributes to learning. Some of the items included in this category are:

- A comprehensive workbook, which provides complete details of the training session. These can have places for the learner to fill in information or else be complete and stand alone as they are. They can be in digital form. Workbooks in one form or another are essential for self-learning, so the learner has the guidelines needed to complete the training.
- Job aids, usually taken from the workplace (e.g., a safety sign placed on a piece of equipment or a flight checklist or computer help menu).
- Posters and signs.
- Mockups of equipment, including cutaways or pieces for training purposes.
- Equipment and systems user manuals.
- Actual equipment.

Preparation for Training

As a trainer, you must be prepared. This can easily require as much effort as developing or delivering the training. If the preparation is not adequate and complete, all your other efforts can quickly be erased. A good rule to use is that any problem that crops up in the training and that is caused by lack of preparation will be fatal.

Use a checklist such as the one in Exhibit 4-7 to help you make sure everything is done and done properly. Checklists will help you select appropriate persons for training, make advance notification to all concerned (learners, trainers, bosses of both, resource persons), determine the adequacy and the amount of the budget, plan so there's a budget reserve (you never know when you might run out of coffee or markers—little things like this can do serious damage), and more.

Having a contingency plan to cover a number of situations that may occur (e.g., cancellation of training, reduction in time to conduct training, loss of media, need to move to a different location) is always a good idea.

Site Selection

Make reservations for space, equipment, travel, lodging, food, and everything else not directly under your control. Include plans for resources to be delivered or designate a person to be responsible for them. Also, make all special accommodations required (particularly those regarding sites and equipment or those required by persons with disabilities or special transportation needs).

Select a site of the appropriate size (too large or too small a venue can cause problems) well in advance, and have backups. From this point on, there are the details: electrical and telephone outlets, a storage room for lengthy sessions (to avoid having to move equipment and materials in and out of the meeting site), accessibility for people with disabilities, location of rest rooms, and so on.

When considering outside facilities, ask whether it is worth the expense. As for the accommodations mentioned earlier, make sure you can rely on the third-party space provider to be able to provide special accommodations for those who need them. It this means you must go to the facility in advance, do not hesitate; the trip may pay off in the long run.

Exhibit 4-7. Training preparation checklist.

Training Session: _____

Date: _____   Location: _____

Number of Participants: _____ In Charge: _____

Item	Required	Completed	Comments
Facilities			
• Room(s) reserved	_____	_____	Note if third party
• Layout specified/ arranged	_____	_____	Send copy to provider
Materials			
• Trainer guide	_____	_____	
• Other materials (list)	_____	_____	
• Facilitator materials	_____	_____	
Equipment			
• Video monitor and DVD player	_____	_____	
• Computer projector	_____	_____	
• Other projector	_____	_____	
• Sound system	_____	_____	
• Miscellaneous (extension cords, outlets, and so on)	_____	_____	
• Boards, markers, and so on	_____	_____	
• Flip chart and tripod	_____	_____	
• Materials for equipment	_____	_____	
Food service (including special requirements)			
• Breaks (coffee, refreshments)	_____	_____	Note how many and when
• Meals	_____	_____	Note how many and when
Personal arrangements			
• Travel (learners, facilitators)	_____	_____	
• Lodging	_____	_____	
• Local travel	_____	_____	
• Special events	_____	_____	
• Recreation	_____	_____	

Room Layout

Training rooms can be laid out in a number of ways, as Exhibit 4-8 shows; the critical element is that the layout fit the situation and be comfortable for participants. The more flexible the room, the better. Bear in mind that some rooms don't lend themselves to certain layouts. For a half-hour session, this might not be a problem, but if learners get sore necks from viewing an inadequately mounted screen over three days of training, the amount of learning will be directly affected—negatively.

Room layout needs must be clearly communicated to the outside facility in advance, with follow-up a must.

There are several things to keep in mind when you select the room (or rooms) for training, although some decisions may be made for you (e.g., if it's to be a computer-generated training, you'll need a space where enough workstations are available):

Exhibit 4-8. Sample room layouts.

Circle or U-shape use for small groups; informal sessions; to encourage interaction

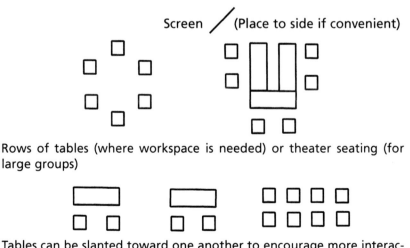

Rows of tables (where workspace is needed) or theater seating (for large groups)

Tables can be slanted toward one another to encourage more interaction.

American Management Association
www.amanet.org

1. Make sure the room is big enough—but a room that's too big can cause problems too (too big, however, is always better than too small).
2. Have working areas for participants to write and place materials if needed.
3. Determine whether ventilation is available, comfortable, and controllable.
4. Consider whether the instructor work area is large enough for materials, media, projectors, and so on.
5. Be sure people in the back can see the screen.
6. Look for interference from other nearby spaces (other training sessions, working crews, and so on). Noise and other distractions tend to ruin a trainer's day, not to mention that of learners.
7. Check on the availability of personal comfort items (restrooms, drinking water, refreshments, and so on).
8. See that lighting is adequate, with control over brightness if needed.

Logistics

This means just what is says. Perhaps you'll only need to have water available for the facilitator, but it must be there. Or you may need to plan for transportation, food (including special meals), lodging (including special accommodations), refreshments, supplies, equipment, shipping training materials, and more. Logistics are included on the preparation checklist (see Exhibit 4-7). These will be identified as you carefully plan the details of the training you've laid out, and outside providers must know what they are.

Pilot Training

If you have the time, conduct a practice run of your training. It can do you a lot of good; for example, it can:

1. Get the rough edges off.
2. Help you adjust times.
3. Identify problem or weak areas, including what needs to be eliminated, redone, or rearranged.

4. Give you some experience delivering the training.
5. Show you how learners might react.

If you have some training experts and representatives from the group scheduled to receive the training, so much the better. Note: A pilot run of a computer-based or online, Web-delivered training program is essential.

Right away you can see the potential problem with pilot training: It takes time and resources, including valuable people time. However, there are things you can do to go through a dress rehearsal of the session. A rule of thumb to use is this: The more people to be trained, the more critical it is to pretest the training.

At least walk through the training in your head or discuss it with someone whose opinion you respect. You can walk through it by yourself if need be—certainly the key parts and those segments you feel least confident about (e.g., a piece of equipment you're unfamiliar with).

For a longer session, do as much of a full-blown walk-through as you can. Remember, there's a lot at stake. If you have custom-designed a program that will be delivered to a large audience over a long period of time, conducting a pilot course becomes essential. Discovering a flaw in the program in the middle of the session attended by 250 people is costly, embarrassing, and unprofessional.

Electronic training to be delivered over the Internet or training to be sent to workstations, both of which become self-learning situations, require that the materials be thoroughly checked out before their dissemination. These materials are the most costly to develop, and there will be no instructor on site to help the learner with any problems that pop up with the material.

Step Five

Deliver Effectively

> *"The learning environment is characterized by physical comfort, mutual trust and respect, mutual helpfulness, freedom of expression, and acceptance."*
>
> —Malcolm Knowles, *The Adult Learner* (2nd ed.), 1978

You've selected how to deliver the training. The next step is where the rubber hits the proverbial road—making it happen. Technology plays a major role in determining how trainers deliver training. Not so long ago, the trainer was the focus of the process. Learning occurred only when the trainer acted. Today, the trainer is a facilitator of a continuous learning process. Coaching, mentoring, and self-directed learning make training a constant in organizational life. This and the fact that a diverse workforce demands different approaches make delivery not only different but more important than ever. How do you facilitate learning, for example, when learners are spread around the globe and can access training at any time they so desire?

Step Five Summary

How well the trainer communicates is the key to ultimate success, whether the trainer is standing before a class or has generated an e-learning session. The best-written, most precise, and most measurable learning objective will be wasted if it isn't communicated properly. Accommodating diversity is a major part of this step. It includes:

- Discussion of trainer as communicator
- Proven communication tips
- Instructions on how to use media
- Instructions on good delivery
- Tips on how to accommodate diversity and multiple generations in training

The Trainer as Communicator

The most obvious form of communication by a trainer is speaking—presenting material to learners in a classroom environment. Yet, verbal communication is but one way a trainer communicates. Written, nonverbal, and electronic means enter the picture, too. Exhibit 5-1 lists some of the ways these forms of communication are used.

To be successful, the trainer must be able to communicate with others during the steps leading up to delivery and later, again through communication, must determine if training has met desired objectives. This means communicating with others during needs assessment and working with subject matter experts during the design and development phases of training. Because communication is such a vital part of training, we look first at the process of communicating, then address how to present training effectively.

Think of communication as it occurs at any point in the training process as a system. Exhibit 5-2 shows it as a closed-loop system; when something is put into it (e.g., a message delivered to a learner), something must come out (e.g., an acknowledgment that the information or skill transmitted in the message will be put to good use). Until this loop is closed, communication hasn't occurred. Note from the exhibit the many pitfalls that can interfere with successful communication. Use this system to keep a clear picture of how to communicate effectively as you deliver training. And don't forget that the message can be delivered nonverbally or in writing. In fact, it's a good idea to pause occasionally to consider whether what you just said (or the exercise just completed, the problem just solved, the role play enacted) communicated what was intended.

Trainer communication skills can be classified into three key

Exhibit 5-1. Ways a trainer communicates.

	Implementation	*When Used*
Verbal	Speaking and listening	• During front-end needs assessment (e.g., interviews and networking with others for ideas and information)
		• During selection processes to speak to experts
		• Making verbal training presentations and speaking to learners during other training activities
		• Obtaining feedback after training
Written	In many formats	• When capturing needs assessment information
		• When writing objectives
		• Communicating with providers and participants
		• During evaluation
Nonverbal	Body language, expression	• During all verbal communication, as well as quiet training times
		• During training exercises
Electronic	E-mail, discussion groups	• Communicating with learners
		• During training exercises

types: verbal, listening, and motivational. All three must be effective if the trainer is to achieve maximum results. (Writing skills are also important and are fundamental to preparation for training, as discussed in Step Four.)

Exhibit 5-2. The communication process: A closed-loop system.

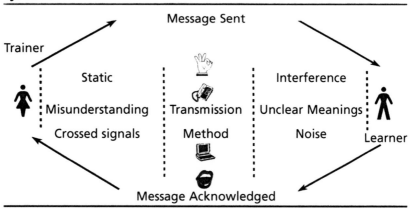

Verbal Skills

Humans have communicated all their lives in some manner, mostly through a symbolic, or written, language. It's this characteristic that sets us apart from other creatures on earth. The fact that we speak to one another as our primary means of communication is usually taken for granted. However, the trainer as presenter can't afford to make assumptions about communicating with learners other than that it must always be done well. Several principles apply to being a good presenter:

- *Keep it simple.* For an audience you may have never met before, keep your presentation simple so that everyone has a maximum opportunity to achieve the learning objectives by being able to comprehend what you are saying. Think also about diversity. More and more learners—valuable members of the workforce— speak English as a second language. Then there's the difference in manners of speech between young and old workers, where the age difference may be 50 years or more.
- *Be clear.* Avoid using words with double meanings. This is where you apply the adult learning principle that learners use their own experiences, which means that the language must be that which they speak and use regularly. This is particularly true when learners from other cultures are present. It can also be a factor with large age differences between learners.

- *Consider how your audience will perceive you.* Adults use their own perceptions to add meaning to the words they hear. This means that stories, analogies, humor, and the like must be perceived by the recipients within the context of the training in general and learning objectives. Think again about age differences and the types of analogies and humor each group of participants might respond to—one group might laugh while the other shakes its collective head.
- *Use imagery.* People have pictures in their heads that have accumulated over their lifetimes. Don't rely on words alone when you can evoke mind pictures that will reinforce learning. This is particularly true when the mind pictures are related to a work setting within the context of the training. This is also where multimodality and exercises assist the trainer dramatically.

Note: Remember that these same principles apply equally to material delivered via computer or the Internet.

Listening Skills

All aspects of training, from needs assessment to after-the-fact evaluation, require that you listen carefully. You must be able to truly hear what people have to say about their needs, assess who is not grasping the material, and comprehend what learners have to say about the completed training.

Following a few simple rules will help you hone your listening skills (bearing in mind that you may be listening face-to-face or electronically via a remote hookup):

- Recognize that the person has something to say and needs to talk it out.
- Genuinely show interest in what the other person has to say.
- Stop whatever it is you're doing to emphasize the previous rule.
- Encourage continued communication on the other person's part. Sometimes all it takes is a nod of your head or a brief word.
- Let the person talk it out, saying everything he or she needs to say.
- Refrain from making judgments.

- Give appropriate feedback.
- Give honest recognition of the other person's feelings, whether it is anger or enthusiasm, disappointment or elation.

Motivational Skills

Motivation was discussed in Step Three, along with various aspects of adult learning theory. Refer to this step for a refresher on motivation and how important it is in communicating during training.

One of your prime responsibilities as facilitator is to go all out to motivate learners. Motivation provides the infrastructure for the communication and training facilitation processes.

As a review, here are selected ways to motivate learners:

1. Give them feedback. Rarely will you be found guilty of giving too much.
2. Always look for positive signs (e.g., that a person has at least part of the answer or is on the right track), and call attention to them.
3. Present all aspects of training in a challenging manner.
4. Encourage participants to stretch their limits during learning.
5. Give simple prizes (e.g., pens, candy, theater tickets) to encourage competition.

How to Give an Effective Presentation

Much has been written and said about how to do a great job making presentations. This material generally follows the same principles found in the eight steps to effective training, starting with being prepared, knowing the audience, and being highly motivated to present. The points identified in Exhibit 5-3 are based on best practice and experience; follow this outline when making any kind of presentation.

One of the exciting elements of delivering training is that there's so much variety available, much of it due to innovations in technology and learning theory, to enhance the process. The challenge is that you must use them well. Included here are tips on using media,

Exhibit 5-3. How to be a successful presenter.

1. Before the presentation:

- Learn everything you can about the participants.
- Have well-stated objectives.
- Think through the questions and reactions participants might have, realizing that dealing effectively with them will remove any doubts and misundersandings. Developing your own questions and responses in advance will be a big help.
- Prepare and practice. There's no substitute for going through every moment of the presentation or session. Use audio, video, and trial runs in front of other people to get advice on how to make improvements.
- Make one last walk-through to make sure all details are attended to, such as room arrangements and logistics. Use a checklist if appropriate, paying attention to any special needs required (e.g., supports for persons with disabilities).

2. During the presentation:

- Be ready to make adjustments as needed, including having standby plans and exercises to use.
- Maintain the proper pace. Do not let your presentation flag or move too fast.
- Stay with the topic by focusing on the objectives established before you started.
- Be aware of your body language and tone of voice. Slumping or speaking in a monotone can undo every good thing you have to say.
- Sometimes you'll have to pick up the presentation, for example, after a long, hearty lunch, so be prepared to step it up a notch to keep things moving, even it it means having a stand-up exercise or a hilarious joke.
- Through your presentation, enthusiasm, and professional actions, let the audience know that your singular purpose is to make the presentation worth their while.

3. After the presentation:

- Get feedback, using formal critique forms and face-to-face questioning of participants. Get feedback from observers, as well.
- Critique your own performance for future improvement (and to pat yourself on the back, too).
- Make it clear that you value feedback and particularly want that of participants.

icebreakers, and humor and on implementing multimodality approaches.

How to Use Media

Most of us have been around DVDs, VCRs, and television monitors for years. What could be so complicated about showing a video during a training session? Writing on a flip chart should be no different from scribbling on a board, right? These aren't trick questions. Video showings that go wrong and flip charts that are unreadable and ripped into shreds are commonplace occurrences for the trainer who doesn't pay attention to them, so, to avoid these problems, apply the general rules in Exhibit 5-4 when using media.

Exhibit 5-4. General rules for using media.

1. *Walk through the media presentation in your mind beforehand* so that you know exactly when and how the media are to be used.
2. *Practice using the media as many times as necessary* to make sure there will be no glitches. Systems are different, and the system you used yesterday may not be the one in the room today.
3. *Don't use a visual aid unless it's readable and concise and makes sense to the viewers.* This includes eliminating the so-called eye chart visuals like those copied from pages of textbooks, visuals with errors on them, and ones that are blemished or faded or otherwise have parts that are unreadable (unless it's a train-the-trainer class and you're demonstrating worst practice).
4. *Never make an excuse for a visual aid.* If you need to make an excuse for it, you shouldn't have used it in the first place. To make apologies will detract from your credibility. The more excuses and apologies you make, the less credible you are.
5. *When a glitch does occur, don't try to cover it up;* rather, move right along, and don't dwell on it. When an apology is necessary, make it (say, "Sorry about that") and move along. Everyone makes mistakes, but keep in mind your role of being the expert and the issue of credibility.
6. *The key to never having to worry about such things as apologies is preparation.* Make sure you are fully ready before you begin.

(continues)

American Management Association
www.amanet.org

Exhibit 5-4. (*continued*)

7. *Have spare support materials available* (lamps for projectors, markers, paper, extension cords, plug adaptors, and so on). (Note: Replacement lamps for computer projectors are expensive.)
8. *When a simple medium will do, use it.*
9. *Don't be afraid to skip use of some media,* particularly visual aids, when you sense it's time to move along. When the audience starts drooping after the first ten of your twenty slides, simply stop and move on to something else. Maybe there'll be some other use for the unused ten pieces, but, if not, it's better to waste them. It's better to have too much material than not enough.
10. Despite your best efforts, problems can occur at any time, and backup systems can fail. *Be prepared by having an alternate plan for delivery*—possibly a couple of alternate plans. For example, use your slides as notes to deliver a manual presentation without visuals if necessary. Use boards to sketch notes and diagrams in lieu of flip charts. The point is that sooner or later, the odds will catch up with you, no matter how hard you try, so be ready. The mark of a good trainer is to make the transition from planned, automated media presentation to backup as seamless as possible, as though you had planned it. The less distraction to the audience, the better, and by no means should you complain or make an issue of the situation. Even if the problem was not your fault, you're the person standing in front of the room, so call as little attention to it as possible.

Each medium has its own unique requirements for best usage. Following are tips on how to use the commonly available training media.

Videos

Videos are common—tens of thousands of them are available commercially—and people are accustomed to seeing them. When you want to use them in training, be sure they are appropriate. Your audience will watch whatever you set before them, being addicted to rectangular shapes and full color as they are, but your choice needs to contribute positively to achieving the learning objectives. Exhibit 5-5 contains tips on making the most of video in you presentation.

Exhibit 5-5. Using video.

1. *Never assume anything*—that the equipment works, that the DVD is properly inserted into the slot (and that it's the correct DVD), that the sound is at proper level, that you know where all the controls are, that you know where the light switch or dimmer is located, that the remote has a good battery (and that you have a spare handy just in case), and so on.
2. *Room lights will probably have to be at least dimmed or partially turned off.*
3. *Always preview any video you use.* This follows the same principle as being sure to read any written material you assigned. If there are any surprises, with context, applicability, or quality, the learners will hold you fully responsible.
4. *If at any time it looks as if there's a problem (e.g., inappropriate materials, quality), stop immediately.* It's better to stop than continue with the problem.
5. *Have the DVD (or tape if it's an old system) inserted into the machine and positioned at the proper start position,* particularly if there are several scenes or programs on the same medium. If there's a several second delay while awaiting the exact starting point, participants may drift away from the material at hand or grumble about your being unprepared and wasting their time.
6. *Use video clips where appropriate.* If a three-minute segment of a video (e.g., one scene or event) will suffice, show just that. Determine at what time you want to start and stop, check it out before the start of the session, and show the short piece. (Caution: If it's a really great video, participants might want to see it all.)
7. *Don't show videos immediately following a meal or at other times when learners might be tired.* This is also good advice for the opening of a new training session—it's better to get learners immediately involved. There are some hard-hitting ones available that might be okay, but the later in the day a video is shown (and especially if it's shown at night), the higher the probability that some folks will nod off. (On the other hand, a good, dull video might serve well as a deep relaxation technique for a stress management class.)
8. Videos add variety to training, so *use them to add insight, to reinforce previously presented material, or to introduce new concepts and ideas.*

(continues)

Exhibit 5-5. (*continued*)

9. *Use videos as an excellent means of presenting cases and examples.* Behavioral-related training uses video effectively to demonstrate proper and improper behaviors (a sort of before-and-after version of desired behaviors).

10. *Make sure the screen is large enough for everyone to see.* Check it out in advance by viewing it from the remotest part of the room.

11. *Tune the picture in advance.*

12. *Adjust sound by getting visual signals from the audience and turn it up or down as needed.* Be careful not to have it come on and blast eardrums. Look toward the people in the back of the room to ensure that they can hear.

13. *Don't stand in front of the monitor or screen.*

14. *Use a remote control, after first making sure it works.* There's nothing more frustrating than trying to make an online adjustment by squatting down in front of the set and finding tiny buttons to push. A remote gives you far more control; you can stay in a position to see exactly what's going on. Anytime there's a problem or any doubt, stop the video immediately.

15. *Don't push any buttons you aren't sure of.* If in doubt, follow the previous instruction, even if it means pulling the power cord out of the socket. Video presentations have been ruined by a facilitator's inadvertently hitting the wrong control.

Flip Charts

Flip charts lend themselves nicely to numerous training situations by capturing on-the-spot ideas and thoughts. Tips to follow when you use them are listed in Exhibit 5-6.

Exhibit 5-6. Using flip charts.

1. *Make sure the tripod or other resting place for the newsprint is sturdy.* If in doubt, try writing in a hurry, pressing down hard as you might do during a busy training session, to make sure the rig is steady. Be careful about using chairs and chalk racks on boards, because they aren't made to hold large pads of paper and can easily give up their contents during crucial times, falling on the floor or on your head.

2. *Use more than one color,* which may take careful thought beforehand and a little practice. For example, ideas might be in blue, with red bullets to set them apart. Special notes might appear in purple or some other contrasting color. Studies have provided information about which colors work best, so, if you care to, dig into this element further.

3. *Be consistent with colors when you do use them.* Otherwise, your efforts might look like a preschool art class.

4. *Practice tearing off pages and taping them to the wall.* This is the key to flip chart use: that you can save thoughts and brilliant ideas for later review. You might even want to start the tear before the session begins, as well as have strips of masking tape fixed to the wall nearby, ready to use. This will speed things up, as well as keep you from looking foolish while ripping sheets in half and dropping things while attempting to tape sheets to the wall. Walk through this ahead of time.

5. *Decide in advance where you want to put up the sheets.*

6. *Have plenty of paper, markers, and tape.* Never go in with only one marker and one roll of tape. One pad of newsprint is okay if it's reasonably full. Use sticky-back paper if possible.

7. *Have more than one pad and tripod for large rooms or for situations where a variety of thoughts and processes will take place.* This way, people in the back of the room won't have to make their way to the front to write on the flip chart. When the training involves groups, each one should have its own tripod, paper, and markers.

8. *Place tripods and pads of paper (or possibly blank sheets taped on a wall) with markers for participants to jot down their comments or thoughts.* For example, individual learners might be asked to write their expectations of the session when they arrive and to then set them aside for later review. There are many ways learners can use flip charts to enhance their involvement and learning.

9. *Print legibly and large enough for everyone to be able to read.* Some trainers who don't print neatly or who are too busy to stop and write may need to recruit a participant to do the writing, or perhaps have an assistant.

10. *Prepare charts in advance where appropriate,* including those where you want learners to fill in blanks, to keep things moving at a livelier pace.

11. *Make sure everyone can see the flip charts,* from both the tripods and the places where they're taped to walls.

35mm Slides

Though there are certainly plenty of old 35mm training slides laying around, digital visuals have replaced them. Even the ones that
are still valid have most likely been digitized, a simple process. If
you have usable 35mm slides, by all means convert them to digital
and continue to use them.

Overhead Transparencies

Transparencies at one time were widely used in training because
they were inexpensive and because it was easy to prepare the visual aids to show in them. You may still find these available, and
there are advantages to using them. There are several ways to generate them, including from hard copy and scanned images. You can
also use blank sheets of acetate and markers to create visuals as you
present training. Some tips for use are shown in Exhibit 5-7.

Exhibit 5-7. Using overhead transparencies.

1. *Use a large font.* The standard is 24-point type, but don't hesitate
   to use a larger one, especially for large audiences. Even people
   with 20-20 vision don't like to squint to read. In fact, no one will
   make much effort to read things that are difficult to see (making
   these people nonparticipants).
2. *Don't put too much information on any one transparency.* A good
   rule to follow is that there should be no more than four or five
   lines of text per visual, using phrases rather than complete sen-
   tences (this holds true for computer-generated slides, too). For
   graphics, use a simplified version of complex diagrams, then additional pieces to show blow-ups of various segments. When in
   doubt, make up the visual, then sit and look at it as if you were
   the participant. The brain can take in only so much at a time, and
   if you make things simple, learning will occur faster.
3. *Turn the machine off when you aren't directly addressing a visual aid,* even if you'll use it again in a minute or so. People will
   keep staring at the bright light projected onto the screen (or wall).
   When you want them to focus on you or someone else or an object
   in the room, turn the machine off, even if there's a transparency
   on it.

4. *Use special markers to write on transparencies,* including for fill-in-the-blanks or to serve as a dryboard, where you generate information from scratch. The advantage is that the transparency can be saved for later use, even for subsequent classes.

5. *Have learners make transparencies of their solutions to group problems.* They can project them onto the screen for discussion and to permit comparison with other group solutions.

6. *Use a pointer or pen as a marker by pointing directly to the desired position on the transparency.* There are also laser and other types of pointers available that can be directed to the appropriate place on the projected image.

7. *Cover all but the item under discussion with a piece of paper,* revealing each subsequent item on the list as you come to it. Otherwise, people will start reading ahead and taking notes while you're still discussing the first item on the list.

8. *Don't stand in front of the screen.*

9. *Don't make excuses for poor visuals.* Don't use them in the first place.

10. *Protect transparencies between uses.* The ink will come off eventually, but the transparency will last longer if you take care of it. There are covers and frames available to both protect visuals and make them easier to handle. At least place a clean piece of paper between them when they are not in use.

11. *Use washable ink markers designed for transparencies.*

Boards

Most of us remember attending school classrooms with chalkboards or whiteboards. These tools still offer the opportunity for spontaneous reaction to learning situations and are invaluable to training and learning sessions. A few rules to keep in mind when using this old standby are identified in Exhibit 5-8.

Exhibit 5-8. Using boards.

1. *Have spare markers (or chalk) and erasers on hand.* Never assume they'll be available unless you have visited the site recently and know they are there.

2. *Don't stand in front of information you've written or drawn on the board.* This is more critical than when using screens, because the

(continues)

Exhibit 5-8. (*continued*)

board is often located directly behind the presenter. Always keep in mind the people in front of you. If you wrote something down (or a learner did), all others present will want to see it, and possibly take it down as notes.

3. ***Practice penmanship before standing before the group.*** Readability is important. When in doubt, spell it out verbally in order to make sure everyone knows what was said.

4. ***Consider using electronic boards.*** They can generate a hard copy (make sure there's plenty of paper on hand) of what is written on them. They work the same as dry marker boards and offer the advantage of capturing what is written.

5. ***Don't erase until you're sure everyone has had a chance to see what has been written and recorded it as needed.***

Computer-Generated Presentation Systems

You need to have some experience when using computer-generated presentations, and you must do it properly. Sometimes you merely need to be familiar with the equipment—how to turn it on, locate the proper presentation, and start it running. Tips on using this training medium are shown in Exhibit 5-9.

Exhibit 5-9. Using computer-based presentation systems.

1. ***Make sure you know how to use the system*** (be thoroughly familiar with it), or else have assistance.

2. ***Try it out first*** to determine the degree of darkness needed and also to see how much light you'll need to operate the system. Great graphics and color soon dissolve on the screen if there's a glare.

3. ***Check out any peripheral equipment that may be involved,*** including locating the nearest electrical outlet, figuring out how long an extension cord may be needed, checking the safety of the cable across the floor, and seeing how well the screen (or wall) works.

4. ***Use a large font and figures.*** Remember, some people may need a little extra help seeing. In other words, unless you have a large screen projector that will magnify the presentation many times, the image will be like that created by projecting a page of text in 12-point type onto the screen—which few people can read.

5. *Keep each slide simple,* no more than five or six lines and simple diagrams.
6. *Have a backup system or manual presentation ready to go*—and be ready to change with little delay, as if you planned it that way.
7. *Rehearse as many times as necessary to ensure a smooth flow.* A pause while you fiddle with a mouse or click on the wrong icon can lose your audience.
8. *Have the presentation set up in advance,* with the first slide ready to go when the class starts.
9. *If you're developing your own presentation,* use only those capabilities of the program you're comfortable with. If you do decide to experiment (e.g., with animation, sound, slide transitions), thoroughly check out the presentation before using it for real.
10. *Take advantage of pointers and remote slide changers for maximum effect.*

Using Icebreakers

Exercises known as icebreakers are meant to do just that: break the ice at the beginning of a session. Because getting sessions started positively is vital to good training, this important exercise form is addressed here. The discussion is equally valid for Step Six, which focuses on getting learners involved. Reasons a trainer might want to use an icebreaker in a training session include helping learners get acquainted, setting the tone or theme for the session, and simply getting people involved immediately.

Getting Learners Acquainted

For a two-hour presentation, introductions should be quick, if done at all. If the learners are to be together for several hours or days, the overall process will be more successful if they meet one another at the outset. They'll either ignore one another if you don't make sure they meet, which could be detrimental to the group process, or else take time to get acquainted anyway, which also will detract from the mission at hand. Bear in mind that learners can instantly communicate with one another, and you, 24/7. This also holds true for e-learning: Learners can use text messaging, e-mail, and blogs to communicate with one another, and this should be encouraged.

Icebreakers can get the job done immediately so that you can move on with the training. This is particularly crucial for group activities. Members need to know what their colleagues have to offer and what roles they'll be willing to play. From the facilitator's viewpoint, each person brings something to learning (occasionally the opposite), and here's where you can find out what it is. It's also a way to identify potential challenges (see Step Six on difficult behaviors).

Setting the Tone or Theme of the Training

This is a process of letting participants quickly learn the purpose of the training and getting things started at a lively pace. For example, a session on diversity could use an icebreaker designed not only to get people acquainted but also to show an element of diversity. Here are some other topics amenable to the use of icebreakers:

1. Communication (all types)
2. Motivation
3. Perception
4. Leadership
5. Self-concepts
6. Problem solving
7. Transfer of training
8. Making changes
9. Team building
10. Thinking in different ways

After participating in an icebreaker exercise, learners will become tuned in to the topic and purpose of the session, and quickly. In doing so, they will have implemented the basic learning premise that adults want to get heavily involved in the process.

Getting People Involved Immediately

Since a key to successful adult learning is active involvement in the process, it's a good idea to get people involved in the training as soon as possible. Staging an icebreaker is an excellent way to accomplish this. It also sends a positive message that you, as facilitator, expect learners to take an active part in the session.

Icebreaker Resources

Experienced trainers have dozens of icebreakers in their bag of learning lore, gathered over the years from numerous sources. Fortunately, there are plenty of resources; the popularity of icebreakers has made it lucrative for many publishers and training materials providers to market them. For example, *Games Trainers Play* by Edward Scannell and John Newstrom, first published in 1980 and still in print because of its popularity, is available. It's the first of a four-book series. There are many other sources of games, as well.

Many icebreakers are made up on the spot, and you don't have to be clever. Having people go around the room and introduce themselves works well, and you can add subtle steps as having them tell a little about themselves (e.g., what book they have recently read, or their favorite computer game). Some representative icebreakers are listed in Exhibit 5-10.

Exhibit 5-10. Sample icebreakers/experiential exercises.

- ***Bingo,*** for getting acquainted. Make up a bingo set that has a variety of items on it, including several that are related to participants (e.g., was born in India, drives a Porsche, has red hair). Participants go around and get the person who fits the box to initial it (limiting the number of times any single person can sign). The first one to get a bingo (up, down, diagonal) wins. The more personalized the form is, the better. Prizes can be awarded if desired.

- ***Two Facts and a Lie,*** for getting acquainted. Each person states three things about himself or herself (e.g., was born in Romania, has six children, once owned an ice cream store). Two of the facts are to be true and one false, but all three are stated as if all were true. The rest of the group guesses which one is incorrect. This game is fun and helps get things off to a good start, while accomplishing the goal of getting people acquainted with one another.

- ***Story Time,*** for listening skills. Participants are arranged in a circle. The person chosen to lead off is given a slip of paper with a brief statement printed on it. The person reads the statement to the second person, whispering in the person's ear. The second must whisper what he or she heard to person number three, and so on down the line. The last person in the circle (next to the originator) states what he or she has heard out aloud, and person number one compares what is said to what is on the sheet of paper. The result is often hilarious. It proves how difficult it is to listen to another human being.

(continues)

Exhibit 5-10. (*continued*)

- **Building a Team.** Participants are put in groups of three to five people and given a task to perform. No instructions are given on how to organize, who is to learn, or anything else. Participants are given a set amount of time to perform the task, such as to write a mission statement for a global electronics firm or determine how to deal with a problem employee. If necessary, provide a short written synopsis of the situation the group is to deal with. The ensuing discussion will uncover the problems with establishing a team and determining who is to be the leader and possibly demonstrate the difficulties in obtaining consensus. The subject matter can also be a significant part of learning.

- **Drawing.** A person is selected to describe a drawing (or picture) on a piece of paper. The drawing can be a grouping of shapes (or anything else not easily perceived). The participants draw what they perceive the person is saying. The participants may not see the drawing and may ask no questions; the presenter can use only words – no hand motions or drawing on a board. Compare and discuss the versions afterwards.

- **Perception.** Show a picture that can be viewed in more than one way or that has more than one meaning. A widely used image shows both an old woman and a young woman within the same drawing. Another is a drawing of two pedestals or glasses side by side, where the two stems form faces. Use this as the lead-in to show how different people have different perceptions.

- **Random video clip.** Show a random video clip, say, from an old TV show or training video, and have people in groups brainstorm how to relate it to the topic at hand. This exercise illustrates thinking ability and can lead to some humorous interpretations.

- **Tube of toothpaste.** Hold up an empty tube of toothpaste. Have participants work in pairs to come up with as many different ways as they can think of in a short time (e.g., three minutes) to remove the last glob of toothpaste from the tube. Acknowledge the more creative ways, possibly giving a prize for the longest list. Add a twist of having people stand up while developing their responses, which will get them moving if they've been sitting a long time.

Note: Other than the first two examples, which focus on getting acquainted, any of the other exercises can be done at any time during a training course. Having them ready is a good way to overcome periods of flagging interest on the part of the participants.

Using Humor

There's nothing like a good joke to loosen things up—that is, if it's an acceptable joke. The problem is that a lot of humor is unacceptable in the workplace, for a number of good reasons. When used properly, though, a bit of lightheartedness can go a long way toward making a training session fun for learners. It's both a good way to start off on the right track (with the audience loosened up after a laugh) and an excellent tonic after a tedious session or large lunch.

Skills training is directly related to workplace success, and the workplace, with all the competition for jobs and sources, can be a highly stressful place. Humor is a good way to help reduce stress anywhere, including in the training environment.

Representative ways to use humor in a training setting are listed in Exhibit 5-11.

Exhibit 5-11. Using humor in training.

- To start off a training session, tell a joke (politically correct, of course), read a short, funny story you've found somewhere, or lead an exercise that is humorous (see some of the exercises listed in Exhibit 5-10).
- During exercises, it helps people see that the facilitator is only human when you can make fun of yourself.
- Several nationally syndicated cartoon strips are directly related to the workplace and often provide the grist for the trainer's humor mill. Get permission to use some of these. If you read the funny papers long enough, you'll find such subjects as diversity, sexual harassment, public speaking, quality management, training, motivation, outsourcing, and more presented through cartoon characters with human characteristics.
- Humor resources, including jokes to use in speaking, are readily available off the shelf. Popular publications also have good materials, and, of course, there are plenty of humor exchange groups to be found online.
- Humorous speakers can make guest appearances during longer training sessions.
- Training programs have taken advantage of the vast supply of old television comedy programs, and it's likely you can find one relevant to your need.

Incorporating Multimodality Approaches

This is a reminder about the importance of this concept. Review Exhibit 3-2 for the details.

Accommodating Diversity and Multiple Generations

This section focuses on the need to accommodate all learners—young, old, native English speakers or those who speak English as a second language, people of different nationalities, different religions, and all the rest—people today are more diverse than ever before. As noted in Step One, Facilitate Learning, the differences between workers today can be great because younger workers bring digital skills to the workplace that may well surpass those of their older colleagues. They also have different expectations from their jobs and different views of their employers. Theory and practice show that people have multiple learning styles (e.g., visual, tactile, musical, numeric), and your job as trainer is to make the most of this fact, which will go a long way to ensuring that learners acquire the new skills they need to be more effective in the workplace.

The approach to take is that everyone is different; if an accommodation of any kind can be made to help an individual learner better, make it. In fact, one of the keys to success for a facilitator is to find ways to accommodate people's needs. We saw in Step One how broad the concept of diversity has become. As the workplace adapts to a continuing trend toward globalization, training must also expand. This means doing different things and training in different ways. If you've been in a meeting or attended a presentation where many attendees were from another culture, you have firsthand experience of what some of these differences are. Analogies are different, not to mention the language used. A story that may be hilarious or thought provoking to one person may be baffling or even shocking to someone from a different background.

Younger workers are accustomed to communicating with people all over the world, using e-mail, instant messaging, and other tools readily available to them. Be sure to encourage this type of communication, and encourage older workers to join in the groups. Increased levels of interpersonal communication, regardless of how it's done, will help your cause. Accommodations for adult learners have already been addressed in Step Two. In the remainder of this step, we will examine accommodations for persons with disabilities, younger workers, and older workers. For a quick review on accommodations, refer to Exhibit 5-12. Also see Appendix A for more details on the various generations.

Exhibit 5-12. How to accommodate diversity in the training environment.

- *Define diversity.* Develop a clear, complete picture and comprehension of true diversity. You must do this first.
- *Biases.* Keep personal biases on the shelf.
- *Focus on individual ability and performance.* Nothing else matters.
- *Consider individual needs.* Always think in terms of accommodations to the greatest extent possible, remembering that many people need to be accommodated to maximize learning.
- *Make accommodations accordingly.* A major accommodation is to adopt a facilitation model that is flexible enough to deal with a diverse group of people. It is described in Step Six.
- *Have a people orientation.* Transcend age, sex, race, and anything else, and train for performance through people, period.

Accommodating Learners with Disabilities

The first point to remember when training learners with disabilities is to be sensitive to their needs. This doesn't mean rushing around trying to move furniture and taking them by the arm every time they start to move; nor does it mean feeling sorry for them and calling attention to their disabilities. Simply treat them like any other participant, and make them feel just as at home as everyone else. The difference is that you may need to do something to accommodate their disability in the training setting—for example, having large-print materials for visually impaired persons and those who may have reading difficulties or a special workstation and computer peripherals for a person with a physical disability.

People often provide their own accommodations; a blind person may bring his or her own Brailler for taking notes, or a person with a learning disability may bring a recording device. When in doubt, always ask the learner what works best.

People with disabilities are a noticeable presence (and sometimes not so noticeable, as you'll read about later on) in the work-place. Your job as trainer is to make the most of the situation and to provide everyone the opportunity to come away with new skills and knowledge. To assist you in this endeavor, we offer a discussion of sensitivity and types of disabilities to assist you in making accommodations. Exhibit 5-13 shows a checklist for accommodating learners with disabilities.

Exhibit 5-13. Checklist for accommodating learners with disabilities.

The following questions are geared to all aspects of the employee development program.

Before training:

☐ Are instructors sensitive to the needs of persons with disabilities?

☐ Do instructors know how to make accommodations for learners who have disabilities (by type of disability, such as hearing or visually impaired)?

☐ Do training materials, delivery methods, and audiovisual devices accommodate disabilities (e.g., open-captioned videos, interpreters for deaf persons, Braille for blind persons, large print)? Note: This applies equally as well to training designed to be delivered online.

☐ Are training facilities accessible (including travel, residential, food, transportation, and recreational facilities)?

☐ Do tests and other methods of measuring performance and training make appropriate accommodations?

☐ Do outside training providers comply with antidiscrimination and accommodation requirements in all aspects of training?

☐ Is language in all documentation nondiscriminatory?

☐ Are any forms used accessible to all persons with disabilities (instructors as well as learners)?

☐ Are records kept for training purposes treated confidentially for medical information for persons with disabilities?

☐ Is a multimodality approach used in delivering training?

During training sessions:

☐ Use multimedia presentations.

☐ Provide written materials in large print and Braille (where needed).

☐ Describe any video, film, computer presentations, or transparencies.

☐ Read all still-projected material (e.g., computer presentations).

☐ Describe any demonstrations or role plays.

☐ Have participants actively participate in hands-on training activities in groups.

☐ Gear testing formats to the learning style of the person with a disability (e.g., Braille version, oral exams, demonstrations).

Sensitivity

The starting place for dealing with learners with disabilities is before training begins. When the training is being planned and announced, and well before the training begins, ask if any attendees need any sort of an accommodation. (Don't ask if anyone has a disability.) It's up to the learner to let you know so that you will be prepared. Make it clear that you will provide reasonable accommodations for those who need them and that they must let you know so you can make the necessary arrangements. This is possibly part of your organization's standard operating procedures.

Being sensitive to persons with disabilities is easy to do if you follow a few simple rules:

1. Always put the person first and the disability second.
2. Don't automatically give assistance. If someone asks for it, willingly give it. When in doubt, you can ask if you might be of assistance, and the person will tell you.
3. Don't lean on a person's wheelchair.
4. Don't pet guide and assistance dogs. They're working and are not to be distracted.
5. Don't set persons with disabilities aside where they are conspicuous. They should be as much a part of the activities as anyone else.
6. Use terms such as *person with a disability, wheelchair user, blind person, deaf person, person with multiple sclerosis,* and so on. Don't use such demeaning terms as *handicapped, crippled, confined to a wheelchair, mute,* and *hard of hearing.*

Types of Disabilities

A wheelchair is the symbol for disabilities. You see it on rest room doors and buses. The category of disabilities, however, includes much more than those that require the use of a wheelchair. General categories include physical disabilities, deafness and impaired hearing, blindness and visual impairment, and nonapparent disabilities (e.g., learning disabilities, mental disabilities, persons with muscular diseases). The point is that for every wheelchair user you might have in a training class, you're likely to have many other people with a variety of disabilities to be accommodated. People with learning disabilities and lower back ailments, neither of which is visible to the facilitator, are a case in point. Estimates are that 10 percent of our population has a learning disability, and lower back ailments are one of the most common workplace disabilities. The responsibility for making accommodations is mutual: You must offer, and it's up to the person with a disability to come forward and let you know what's needed. Exhibit 5-14 and the following discussion provide guidance for making accommodations for people with various disabilities.

Physical Disabilities

Wheelchair users may require a lower workstation. Make sure aisles are wide enough (usually 42 inches is required) for maneuverability. Most facilities accommodate wheelchairs, but never assume that yours is accessible; check it out to be sure. Disability support groups and rehabilitation programs can offer expert advice on how accessible your space is. Computers and related equipment may need to be equipped with assistive devices (e.g., alternative input devices such as voice-activated software).

The Deaf and the Hearing Impaired

Deaf and hearing-impaired people may require an interpreter who is qualified in American Sign Language (ASL). The facilitator should always face the audience when speaking. Don't speak to the interpreter when conversing with a deaf person. Rather, speak directly to the one who's deaf. Many deaf and hearing-impaired people are adept at lip reading. Also be conscious of lighting, and avoid having bright lights behind a speaker. Videos must have captioning. Sound amplification devices are helpful for those who are hearing impaired.

Exhibit 5-14. Training tips for accommodating people with disabilities.

1. *Physical disabilities*
   - Wheelchair users may require a lower workstation.
   - Aisles should be wide enough (42 inches or wider) to permit maneuverability.
   - Most facilities accommodate wheelchairs, but you should never assume they do. Check them out to be sure.
   - Disability support groups and rehabilitation programs can offer expert advice on how accessible your space is.
   - Computers and related equipment may need assistive devices (alternate input, such as voice activation devices).

2. *Deaf and hearing impaired*
   - Deaf and hearing-impaired persons may require an interpreter who's qualified in American Sign Language (ASL).
   - The facilitator should always face the audience when speaking.
   - Don't speak to the interpreter when conversing with a deaf person. Rather, speak directly to the one who's deaf.
   - Many deaf and hearing-impaired people are adept at lip reading.
   - Be conscious of lighting, and avoid having bright lights behind a speaker.
   - Videos must have captioning.
   - Sound amplification devices are helpful for those who are hearing impaired.

3. *Blind and visually impaired*
   - One of the main accommodations for a blind person is to explain what is happening in videos and to read every word on every visual aid.
   - If there's a role play, describe what the participants are doing.
   - Braille or recordings may be appropriate for training materials. So are recording devices and players for recording presentations.
   - For visually impaired persons, large print and terminals that enlarge printed tpe and project it onto the screen are two common accommodations.

4. *Nonapparent disabilities*
   - These disabilities cover a wide spectrum but can be accommodated in a number of ways.
   - For people who have medical conditions such as cancer or lower-back conditions, flexibility in scheduling and attendance may be in order (e.g., so that the person can rest for brief periods or take prescribed treatment).

(continues)

Exhibit 5-14. (*continued*)

- Learning disabilities related to difficulties in reading, writing, spelling, computing, attention span, and organizing abilities may require alternative formats, such as recording devices for training sessions, alternative methods of taking tests, additional time to complete portions of training, prerecorded materials, note takers, and other assistance in the learning process.

The Blind and the Visually Impaired

One of the main accommodations for a blind person is to explain what is happening in videos and to read every word on every visual aid. If there is a role play, describe what the participants are doing. Braille texts or recordings may be appropriate forms for training materials, and recorders can be useful for recording presentations. For visually impaired persons, large-print materials and terminals that enlarge printed type and project it onto the screen are two common accommodations.

Nonapparent Disabilities

Nonapparent disabilities cover a wide spectrum but can be accommodated in a number of ways. For people who have medical conditions, such as cancer or lower back pain, flexibility in scheduling and attendance may be in order (e.g., so the person can rest for brief periods or take prescribed treatment). For people with learning disabilities—difficulties in reading, writing, spelling, or computing; shortened attention spans; and difficulty in organizing—alternative formats may be needed, such as recording devices for training sessions, alternative methods of taking tests, additional time to complete portions of training, prerecording materials, and the use of note takers.

Dealing with Younger Participants

The main consideration for younger learners is that they have shorter attention spans, spend much time with handheld devices, probably don't read as much, and think in terms of "sound bytes" —those short bursts of information associated with watching television and playing video games for hours at a time. A characteristic of a large number of younger workers is that they can do many things at once, and, in fact, some aren't happy unless multitasking (e.g., watching some combination of television programs, reading the streamers across the bottom of the screen, text messaging, listening to music, and perhaps eating dinner). Simply bear in mind that younger learners will view what you do as a trainer in a very different light from most other learners.

Dealing with Older Participants

There are a number of myths about older adults, all of them untrue. Learning ability doesn't drop as people grow older; older people want to continue working (many because they have to); and they show up on time, produce as much, and stay at work just as long as younger workers. Most important, older people are proving to be adaptable; they're willing to learn new skills mandatory to workplace—and organization—success. It's important that trainers recognize that the number of older learners participating in training will continue to grow as the population grows older, so it's important to avoid stereotyping them. Treat older learners the same as everyone else; in fact, take advantage of their in-depth work experiences in training.

One of the ways you can take advantage of having older learners in the group is to call on them often during training so that they can share their experience and knowledge. Even before training starts, consult with them on how to develop meaningful exercises and other activities during the training. Also, be aware that older adults may need accommodations because of visual and hearing losses. Exhibit 5-15 lists some tips you can use when dealing with younger and older workers in a training environment.

Exhibit 5-15. Tips for dealing with younger and older learners in a training environment.

1. Show respect for all learners, regardless of age or other differences.
2. Recognize that people are different and that this is perfectly okay.
3. Recognize that younger learners have learning styles that are technology based and prefer shorter segments, while older workers prefer more traditional forms of learning.

(continues)

Exhibit 5-15. (*continued*)

4. Assume that *all* learners will be motivated to succeed in the training session because the result will increase their value to the organization.
5. Stimulate cooperation and interaction between older and younger workers (e.g., get a younger worker to assist an older worker if the latter is not knowledgeable about the technology being used to deliver the training).
6. Allow learners, particularly younger ones, to take control of their learning to the greatest extent practicable.
7. Encourage learners, particularly younger ones, to identify their strengths and weaknesses, and focus on strengths.
8. Build as much flexibility into the training as possible, including multiple delivery methods where possible, short segments, and, generally, a blended approach.
9. Include as much variety as possible in order for all learners to find something they are comfortable with.

Conclusion

Trainers are blessed with an enormous amount of material—checklists, books, journals, workshops, and more—to help them ply their trade. Some may think *overblessed* is a better word because there's so much information inundating them, with more becoming available each day. One of the keys to success in filtering so much information is to look ahead at the training you'll be doing and identify a few significant areas for review. For example, if you know older workers will be attending the training session, read up on some of the tips in this step and possibly do a Web search or contact someone who has had experience with this age group. If you'll be doing a lot of classroom presentation, review the material regarding speaking and presenting in this step, and possibly get a book on humor (or locate a Web site of appropriate humor) and exercises to conduct in order to make your presentation as interesting as possible. For one last reminder before going on to the next step, Exhibit 5-16 lists a number of do's and don'ts for trainers. Use this as a last-minute check before stepping onto the platform to start your session.

Exhibit 5-16. Do's and don'ts for trainers.

Do:
- Speak clearly.
- Make eye contact.
- Get learners involved.
- Use learners' names.
- Keep interest up through changing your tone of voice.
- Get, and give, constant feedback.
- Be enthusiastic. If this is tough, take acting lessons.
- Be prepared.
- Use specific questions to determine if learning is taking place.
- Observe breakout groups. They miss you when you don't and may do something else.
- Be alert for those who need a little extra help—and give it to them.
- Move around.
- Accommodate each individual to the greatest extent possible.
- Use equipment and aids as if you've been doing this all your life—even if it's the first time.
- Set and observe time periods. The only acceptable time change is to end early.
- Dress appropriately.

Don't
- Mumble.
- Waste words ("you know," "I'm like," "uh").
- Read from notes.
- Take part in private conversations during sessions.
- Talk to visual aids.
- Lecture or preach.
- Ignore questions.
- Pace up and down.
- Turn your back to the audience while speaking.
- Stand in front of visual aids.
- Forget to make eye contact.
- Forget that there are people on both sides and in back of the room.
- Chew gum or food during a session.
- Give people busywork in order to fill up the allotted time.
- Stay in one position for long periods (including being glued to the

(continues)

Exhibit 5-16. (*continued*)

podium; some rooms have automatic light shut-offs—think how embarrassing it would be if the lights went out during your session).

- Put your hands in your pockets, cross them in front of you, or use them excessively.

- Wear distracting attire.

Step Six

Get Learners Involved

"Workplace training and technology will need to fit both the learning styles and lifestyles of a multigenerational workforce."

—Janice Ware, Rosemary Craft, and Steve Kerschenbaum,
American Society for Training and Development, 2007

Get learners involved in the learning process and you'll be a successful trainer. When an adult learner is mentally and physically dedicated to learning, learning will take place—and learning will go up in proportion to the learner's degree of involvement.

You have read about a number of ideas for getting learners involved. This step lays out a wide range of specific techniques and tools for you. When appropriate, techniques have been associated with types of learning situations to help you choose the best one for your needs. For this reason, this step goes hand in hand with Step Four, which focuses on selecting delivery methods and media. Sometimes experimentation is okay. Think of a way to get learners involved, and try it out. You'll be able to tell right away if it's working. If it's not, move on to something else. Also, it's always a good idea—perhaps you can make it mandatory with all your training—to have backup exercises, questions, techniques, and so on ready to go just in case.

American Management Association
www.amanet.org

Step Six Summary

A vital part of involvement is group dynamics and actions. Much training takes place in groups, particularly in teams, to replicate actual workplace environments. To deliver training most effectively, the trainer must have a good knowledge of group dynamics and be adept at facilitating group learning. Included within this step are:

- Discussion of group activities
- Tips for dealing with a variety of group situations
- Techniques for working with groups
- Action learning
- Online learning involvement

Working with Groups

The training facilitator must be adept at working successfully with groups of all sizes. Knowledge of group dynamics and the ability to deal with problem behaviors within groups are essential facilitator skills. Fortunately, applying a few proven tips will lead you to success in working with groups.

Group Dynamics

Groups provide an excellent, efficient means to get things done—but they're also likely to present their share of challenges. Knowing how to deal with groups is essential to the achievement of the ultimate learning objective. What you must remember is that groups, like individuals, have minds of their own, with motivations, likes, dislikes, objectives, standards, and desires. This holds true even if members have never seen one another before coming to the training session.

Groups are formed for specific purposes, whether formal or informal, and you must work successfully with them. Here are a few key items to keep in mind:

- Groups have goals, and in a training situation, the goals must coincide with those of the training at hand for maximum learning to take place.

- Groups have norms. You've probably been in a group when you wanted to speak up but had the feeling that the group didn't want you to. Perhaps the norm was to make the leader work hard for results, or perhaps the newcomer was expected to keep silent and in the background until proper dues were paid.
- Groups have some sort of structure; it can be informal if a random group has been drawn together for training purposes.
- Individual group members have specific roles to fill. Perhaps one person has been chosen as the unofficial leader, and everything must go through him or her. Or perhaps there are role conflicts that must be resolved before the group's goal can be achieved, such as when two learners want to be leader.
- People within a group exhibit certain behaviors depending on what they expect to get out of the group. For example, people who want to establish themselves as experts may try to dominate training sessions.
- Younger workers in groups are likely to continue their intergroup communication through many rapid and readily available forms of everyday technology.

Keep these rules in mind to achieve a high success rate and to forestall problems when dealing with training groups in general. They are less influential when the session is short or the group is ad hoc and not a cohesive work team brought in for training. Nevertheless, group behavior plays a strong role in everything that goes on during training.

Using Small Groups

Sometimes referred to as *breakout groups*, these small groups consist of people who have been chosen by the trainer to be brought together during a training session. Small groups can be used for case studies, exercises, problem solving, icebreakers, debates, or games. You can have all groups deal with the same problem or exercise or use different exercises for each group. In longer sessions, you might want to re-form groups so that participants will have the experience of working with different people. This can add much needed freshness when there's a lot of group activity.

To form groups, have participants count off up to the number of groups desired (e.g., one to five), with all people with the same number coming together in one group (this is a good technique to use when you want to make sure certain learners are separated into different groups). Or you can divide into groups before the training begins.

Dealing with Difficult Behaviors

There's always the possibility that some member in a training group will find a way to go against the grain. When it comes to training, this person usually can't be ignored. Interruptions to a tightly scheduled training session detract from the group's ability to achieve its objectives. Every time there's a delay, lost time accumulates and makes it more difficult to recover the momentum.

Among the skills you need are those for dealing with disruptive individuals. They come in all types and can cause grief in a number of ways. Fortunately, they're usually in the minority, and there are ways to deal with them. Before getting into special situations, there are three cardinal rules to follow:

Never put anybody down (i.e., call attention to a trainee's behavior or chastise a trainee in any way). It's okay to be firm, but always be polite and understanding. Loss of credibility as a facilitator goes hand in hand with loss of one's cool in a training session.

However people act and whatever they do, remember that they have their reasons. You're not in a position to make judgments. You therefore need to respect that there's a reason for the behavior.

Treat learners with dignity and respect at all times.

Monopolizers, quiet ones, digressers, chatterboxes, and disruptive people are common problems for group leaders. By assuming that you may face any and all of these in any training situation—and by being prepared to deal with them—you can ensure that your training sessions go smoothly. Also, realize that these people may not be aware that their behavior is causing a problem. Anticipating problematic behaviors allows you to deal faster and more positively with these behaviors when they occur and to promote learning. Exhibit 6-1 gives tips for handling them.

Exhibit 6-1. Tips for handling difficult behaviors in groups.

1. *Monopolizers*
- Recognize the person's contribution; then call on someone else.
- Intervene, thank the person for the answer; then say you want to give someone else a chance.
- Institute a practice of having people hold up their hands to respond; then ignore the monopolizer's hand most of the time.
- Call on specific individuals, rather than allowing people to speak spontaneously.

2. *Quiet Ones*
- Let it be known at the beginning that you appreciate and expect responses from everyone present.
- Call on the quiet ones, giving advance warning that you will do so.
- Start with easy questions, and work up to more difficult ones.
- Ask a controversial question or take a controversial position (but be careful).

3. *Digressers*
- Reply that the question or comment is beyond the scope of the session, but you'll be happy to discuss it during a break or when the session is over.
- Keep reminding participants of the main topic so that they won't lose sight of it.
- When uncertain of how to respond, make a note and tell the person that you'll give the question some thought (or research it, call an expert, or whatever else is appropriate) and get back to him or her. In this case, you may have to say that you're unprepared to deal with the question or comment at this time but will respond later.

4. *Chatterboxes*
- Stop the presentation and wait for the people engaged in a private conversation to realize they're disrupting the class. Often this is all it takes, particularly if they don't realize they are causing a problem for others.
- If the behavior persists, politely interrupt and ask what it was the person said, as if you thought he or she was speaking to the group, in the hope that the person will apologize or at least be quiet.
- Interrupt and politely ask those having the private conversation to put it off until the break; then state when the break will be.
- It may become necessary to confront them (politely, of course) at a break and ask them to stop. If there is something they must talk about, suggest they go outside and carry on the conversation, but remind them of the importance of being present at the training.

(continues)

Exhibit 6-1. (*continued*)

---

5. *Disrupters*

- Stop and tell the person you understand his or her concern (or whatever other comment fits the situation) and will gladly discuss the matter after the session.
- Break into a new activity to cut off further disruptive action.
- Ask the person to participate in an exercise or assist in a training task (i.e., put this person in charge of some phase of the learning process).
- Sometimes you may need to engage in direct confrontation, despite your best efforts to avoid it. Tell the person that it's imperative that the session continue and that you would like to discuss the problem later. If it becomes necessary, suspend the training session temporarily and deal with the problem, even it means contacting someone who can take action for you. This should be done outside the training area, away from other learners. Fortunately, being assertive and insisting, in a positive, tactful way, usually get things back on track.

The Monopolizers

There's an excellent possibility that in any group of people, at least one individual will be exceptionally knowledgeable about the session topic. This person will have much to say and can easily take too much time saying it. Some people simply like to talk a lot, and a training session gives them a captive audience.

Whether the person really is unusually knowledgeable or simply likes to talk, he or she can detract from your mission to achieve specified learning objectives. Considering how tight schedules and budgets are, every minute must count. In other words, you must do something to prevent monopolizers from taking over a session and, more important, from keeping others from being able to participate.

Sometimes the other members of the group let the monopolizer know, in subtle or not-so-subtle ways, to be quiet. You shouldn't sit back and wait for this to happen, but if it does, it's usually okay to let it be so—without encouraging it. In other words, let the group tend to its own business, and intervene only if it looks as if there might be a problem.

The Quiet Ones

One of the most frustrating moments for a trainer is a silent response to a challenging, well-developed question. There are plenty of reasons for lack of response: Perhaps no one knows the answer; perhaps no one understood the question or request; perhaps the group is bored or believes the question or response is beneath them or is unimportant; or perhaps there is a monopolizer in the group and other members are intimidated to the point of not bothering to respond. Or perhaps they just don't want to say anything (e.g., they're ready to go home and don't want to prolong the session)—or they simply don't care.

The Digressers

The digresser is the person who takes the meeting down side roads and gets off onto topics that have little, if anything, to do with the learning objectives. The behavior isn't always intentional, either. In fact, it's quite easy to go off on a tangent and get sidetracked from the original purpose. People bring their own agendas to the training session. The ability to keep things on track is one of the many talents of good meeting leaders and trainers. It's of little matter whether the digression is intentional; it must be dealt with immediately. Wasted time adds up quickly, especially in the minds of participants.

The Kibitzers

Every group has these people—those who, usually from vantage points toward the back or side of the room, whisper into one another's ears during a presentation. There's a more severe version of this: Those who don't whisper as they talk about everything from what they think of the training (which is probably not very much) to where they will go for lunch at the break (if it will ever get to that time). The behavior can be innocent, as when two people have work business to attend to and don't know when there will be time later to exchange information, to thoughtless, as when the kibitzers don't care if they disrupt. Either way, it's distracting to the others.

The Disrupters

This is a general category of people who interfere in one way or
another, by questioning everything you say or propose, challenging
your credibility, making comments that the training is a waste of
time, asking questions about material that was covered earlier in the
session, refusing to participate or do what has been asked, and so on.
They may disrupt only briefly, or their mission may appear to be to
disrupt the entire proceedings. Perhaps the person is a skeptic about
training in general or about the new skills being offered in the training. Maybe the person didn't want to be part of the session in the
first place (and this could be for good reason, so don't be too quick
to judge). Possibly the person has a personal problem and can't fully
enter into the training. And it could be that the person is naturally
cantankerous and disruptive by nature. Whatever the reason for the
behavior, too much of it will ruin the process for everyone.

Dealing with disrupters is a challenge under any circumstances.
Though it might seem okay simply to put them in their place, doing
so is likely to cause others to doubt your ability to work well under
pressure and therefore to jeopardize your credibility as a trainer.
Yet, letting the behavior go on is unthinkable, so you must take
action.

Dealing with Devices

Workers from Generations X and Y may well come to a training
class with a cell phone strapped to one side, a handheld device at-
tached to the other, earphones on, and a laptop stuffed into their
backpack. Their hands often are busy fiddling with a device no matter what else they're doing. They are multitaskers, able to do several
things (e.g., conducting research on a laptop while sitting in a class,
text messaging a friend in another part of the building, and playing
a computer game on the hand-held device). The question is: Is this
okay in a standard classroom setting? The best answer is no—any
one of these devices can disturb others in the class (unless all are at
it), and, as in the theater, group members should be asked not to use
them during the training. This isn't easy, especially if the trainees
are all managers and you're a junior trainer.

It's not just young workers who are never without their devices.
We have all grown dependent on electronic devices, especially if

they make our lives easier. Some technological innovations, such as e-mail and text messaging, are integral parts of everyday work. But ringing cell phones, sounds from any device, and the distraction of seeing the person beside you busy doing something other than paying attention to the class all detract from the training. One way to take some of the pressure off you as trainer is for the company to have a policy prohibiting devices that could detract from training. If it's organizational policy, so much the better.

Techniques for Getting Learners Involved

Trainers, teachers, and researchers have given us many ways to get learners involved. They work well, they're fun, and they help deliver training that stresses all the senses and motivations of learners. Together they provide quite a powerful set of techniques for the facilitator. (These techniques are summarized in Exhibit 6-2.) You'll note that there's some overlap with material in other steps, which reflects the integrative, systems aspect of training.

Asking Questions

As demonstrated by the Greek philosopher Socrates, asking questions is one of the oldest and most effective ways to help others learn and grow. With modern technology and enormous strides made into learning how people learn, this technique remains one of the trainer's greatest tools. The ability to ask probing questions that cause learners to open their minds and focus on the topic under discussion is one of the best assets you can have. It's the same essential skill managers use to probe deeply into organization issues. By asking questions, you will know at all times if learning is taking place.

You can use questions in a number of ways. The most direct way is to ask questions at intervals throughout the training session, even if it's primarily an experiential session rather than a presentation. Ask questions about everything. Rather than provide information, present it as a question. You can also use written questions, as in a test. Also, provide a list of specific questions to be answered for cases and similar exercises. It'll keep learning on target and keep discussion groups focused. Questions prepared in advance will always serve you well.

Exhibit 6-2. Techniques for interacting with learners: A summary.

1. *Ask questions.*
   - Review questions prepared in advance.
2. *Conduct experiential exercises.*
   - Use all types.
   - It's possible to accomplish many learning objectives entirely through exercises, where learners can experiment, practice, then demonstrate proficiency.
3. *Conduct role plays.*
   - Use for a variety of situations.
   - Follow the rules.
4. *Learn each learner's name and use it.*
   - Spend time at the beginning of the training session working on names—in advance if you have the names.
   - Repeat group members' names as they introduce themselves.
   - Spell the names.
   - Use name tags or name table tents.
   - Practice names at the beginning of subsequent sessions.
   - Let learners know you care about them and want to get their names right.
5. *Provide feedback during class.*
   - Make sure learners always have plenty of time to raise questions.
   - Be available before and after sessions, as well as during breaks and outside class hours. Use e-mail and text messaging where appropriate.
   - Conduct formal surveys to find out problems, questions, and expectations. Do this in writing, so learners must respond, but make these surveys anonymous.
   - Learners may respond to this tack even if they have questions they won't ask in class.
6. *Turn instruction over to learners.*
   - Let them prepare and deliver parts or all of sessions.
   - When a learner asks a question, have another learner answer it.
7. *Let learners perform demonstrations.*
   - Do this even if they've never seen the equipment before. Help them out if necessary.
   - Turn demonstrations into exercises, and give learners time to prepare.

8. *Incorporate writing exercises.*
   - Writing reinforces learning.
   - Use a variety of exercise types.
   - Use blogs.
9. *Make learning contracts.*
   - People respect contracts.
   - Make contracts in writing, even informal ones.
   - Meet individually with each learner and determine what he or she expects from training and from you.
10. *Use instruments to learn more about learners.*
   - Learning, trainer, and involvement styles help identify important information about individuals.
   - Instruction can be altered to accommodate these styles where appropriate.
   - Learning is made more interesting if learners learn something new or confirm something about themselves.
11. *Hold individual meetings.*
   - Discuss progress and expectations.
   - Provide counseling to those learners needing it (e.g., regarding the training or personal situations that affect the training).
   - Establish learning contracts.
   - Get acquainted.
12. *Make training real time and action oriented.*
   - Add realism.
   - Use action learning, with actual workplace situations.
   - Use a team approach, emphasizing diversity.

Open-Ended and Closed Questions

Closed questions most likely have only one correct answer (e.g., true or false, yes or no, or a direct fact answer). They work well during training sessions to help the trainer figure out if learners are paying attention and the facilitator is getting the job done. *Open-ended questions* require more thought from the respondent, and the learner can answer in his or her own words. Such questions probe more deeply into how well learning objectives are being met, though they are more difficult to critique because they are more subjective. For example, during a supervisory training session, asking the learner to identify ways to discipline a worker, then to explain why a particular choice was made, requires a deeper level of thinking and answering—a value of open-ended questioning.

The better type of questions, as any successful sales representative will tell you, are open-ended ones. These are ones that begin with the proverbial "who, what, where, when, why, how, and if," the so-called five W's, H, and I. They require thought to answer.

Direct and Indirect Questions

You can either ask a specific person to answer a question *(direct)* or present it to the entire group *(indirect)* for anyone to try to answer. Sometimes both approaches are required. For example, if learners seem reluctant to respond to indirect questions, first ask the question in general, then turn to a particular learner and ask for an answer. That way, you are giving advance warning, and the person can start formulating an answer. Sometimes indirect questions can be used to introduce a topic and nudge the learners to start thinking, though no answer is expected.

How to Ask Questions

Here is a list of things you should know about asking questions:

1. Let learners know up front that you will ask a lot of questions, that you expect them to provide answers, and that it is okay if the answers are sometimes wrong.
2. Use open-ended questions (who, what, where, when, why, how, and if) , because they work best.
3. Ask questions that make people think, which is what open-ended ones will do.
4. Ask questions that learners can probably answer correctly. The greater the chance a learner has of answering a question correctly, the more effective it will be. A rule to use is to ensure a 90 percent chance the learner will get the correct answer.
5. Give credit for partial answers.
6. Never make fun of an answer, unless the person providing the answer laughs first.

7. Ask questions at the beginning of the session. The answers will help you determine where learners stand and show how much knowledge they already have.
8. Ask questions regularly during the session to determine if learning is occurring, as well as to give you a sense if it's time to change the pace.
9. Use questions at the end of a session segment as a way to summarize the material and determine if it has been successful.
10. Use a variety of types of questions, including direct and indirect ones. (It's okay to ask simple ones that have yes or no answers or that look for specific pieces of information as answers to provide variety. These simpler questions also help decrease the anxiety when the material is difficult.)
11. First address a question to the entire group, so all participants can start thinking of the answer. Then single out an individual to provide the answer.
12. Give plenty of time for the person to respond.
13. Give hints if they will help. This communicates that you sincerely want the person to learn and that it is okay to not always have the answers.
14. Give everyone a chance to answer during the course of a lesson. Calling on specific people is a way to make the questioning fair and equal for everyone. You can go down the rows sometimes to ensure uniformity.
15. Try to find something positive about every answer that is given.
16. Do your best not to answer the question yourself. This can be a challenge if the group is quiet or slow to respond.
17. When you make a mistake during questioning (and human nature being what it is, it will certainly happen sooner or later), admit it.
18. Keep questions and the process of asking them as simple as possible (i.e., never use trick questions).

Learners may ask questions. When they do:

1. Get someone else to answer.
2. Solicit comments.
3. Don't evade the question.
4. Don't engage in put-downs.

5. Deal with an irrelevant question from a learner by politely stating that it isn't pertinent or that you'll answer it at the break.
6. If a learner is asking a question to achieve something else, try to rephrase the question to a more legitimate one.
7. If the question indicates that a person is lost, find a way to help that person out (e.g., during a break).

Role Playing

Drama has a way of getting people absorbed in the situation. You can add drama to your training session in a number of ways, including through video and exercises or, more directly, through role plays. You'll need time to prepare and participants who are willing to do their best to take on the assigned roles.

Role plays are excellent for demonstrating behaviors and helping learners gain firsthand experience in what it feels like to be on the receiving end of those behaviors. They can be used to show both positive and negative situations, and sometimes both for comparison purposes. Role plays are useful for training in a number of areas:

- Sales training, to illustrate prospective client behaviors and how trainees can turn them to advantage
- Diversity training, in which learners take on roles of various groups
- Communications training, to demonstrate a range of communications techniques, from listening skills to body language
- Management development, to demonstrate desired managerial situations and how to deal with them (e.g., how to be a coach or mentor)
- Interview training, so that interviewers learn how to conduct interviews according to legal and other guidelines
- Conflict management, for dealing with customer complaints and internal conflicts

When you conduct role plays, pay attention to these guidelines:

- Carefully plan how they're to be used.
- Make it clear what's expected of participants (e.g., saying that everyone is to participate, that it's okay and expected that they

might have to work at it to carefully move into the process). It's good to do this before the training begins to avoid surprises.

- Create a relaxed, nonthreatening atmosphere so that participants will feel at ease taking on roles.
- Be aware that some people have difficulty getting into playing roles. If encouragement doesn't work, don't force someone to play a role.
- Give participants as much background information as possible to help them assume their respected roles.

Learning Names and Using Them

Perhaps you've known someone who could walk into a room and meet twenty strangers, then a short time later go around the room and call each person by name without a mistake. We're not all like that, but there are a number of tricks to learning names for training purposes. Because people respond much more positively when you address them by name, knowing names is vital. In fact, you may discover that some people won't say a word until you say their name. If you stop to think about this, you will realize that you too feel much better about any situation when the people around you, especially the leader or facilitator, can associate your face with the proper name. Personalization takes a lot of discomfort out of any situation, including training settings. (This gets back to the reason that icebreakers can be so valuable.)

There are books and courses available to teach you techniques for remembering names if you're interested. And here are some easy-to-use tips:

- Get a list of the participants before the training begins and become familiar with their names. Learn as much as you can about the participants (e.g., where they're from, what they do, any positive information you've heard about them, and what expertise you might be able to count on from them).
- Associate specific things about each person with the name (e.g., Joe who couldn't find a parking space, or Sally from accounting, which could be information gleaned from a getting-acquainted exercise).
- Spend time at the beginning of the session (unless it's a short one) learning names (e.g., calling them out and repeating each one several times).

- When there are multiple sessions, go over names at the beginning of each one. This repetition helps you learn them and shows learners that you care enough to learn their names.
- Repeat names several times at the start of the session.
- Spell names out as you say them.
- Use name tags.
- Use name cards at the workstations, such as name tents (name cards folded into a V shape).

Providing Feedback During Training

This sounds simple, and it is. However, in the middle of a busy training session, you may forget to do it. Providing feedback can be as simple as thanking someone for a good answer to a question, accompanied by a smile. After each exercise, tell the learners how well they did. If they didn't do well, soften your feedback by saying that they got the job done but could do better, and you're sure they will next time. Use praise lavishly, and definitely when a response is excellent.

Here are some ways to provide feedback:

- Walk around the room during group exercises, and comment on what people are doing. They need to know you're interested.
- Use body language to show approval (e.g., smile to show approval when someone has responded to a question, and shake your head up and down or applaud).
- Encourage applause when a person or group has made a presentation. Try to do this always in more formal situations, such as when a learner has given a talk during a verbal communication course or a group has presented a solution to a case study.
- Write notes and comments on written work completed during the session.
- Summarize each segment of a session, and include it in the summary comments. Your comments will let people know how they're doing.
- Stop people as they are leaving or walking down the hall during a break and offer feedback—even if just a word or two.
- Give feedback promptly. This way it's easier to remember.
- Provide certificates or letters of completion when training is over (sending copies to their supervisors when appropriate—these could become important additions to their personnel records).

Turning Instruction Over to Learners

Be careful with this technique. Never give up responsibility for facilitating the process, but use it to keep learners involved. One way to do this is to ask small groups to prepare a brief presentation and deliver it to the rest of the class or to perform an exercise or demonstration. Be sure necessary reference materials are readily available so that the presenters can do a thorough job of preparing. Case studies also provide a method for learners to take over a portion of the instruction. The learners, rather than the facilitators, can state the lessons learned from solving a case or exercise. Yet another way to turn over instruction is to have a learner provide the answer when another learner asks a question.

To see how to turn instruction over to learners, consider a diversity training class. If the objective is for learners to conduct themselves properly in a meeting with people from different cultures, learners should be asked to prepare two demonstration meetings: one showing how *not* to act during such a meeting (e.g., pushing for immediate action with someone from a culture that always goes through a series of social actions first) and the other showing how to act patiently and properly. In preparation for the sessions, learners should be provided with information on key points of the culture represented in the example.

Letting Learners Perform Demonstrations

This is similar to the previous idea. Often in technical training (e.g., computer-related or technical maintenance training), it's necessary to demonstrate the correct way to load a system or perform a specific task so that learners can see the correct procedure before doing it themselves. In this situation, you might have a system set up in front of the room or perhaps use a projection onto a large display. Rather than going through the steps yourself, ask a learner to come forward and do the task. You are sending a message to the class that the task will be easy for them to master and that you're confident about their ability. When using this method, be sure to let participants know it's okay to make mistakes. In fact, having learners perform demonstrations is an excellent way for them to see that making mistakes is okay and no harm is done—and that this is the place to learn from their mistakes.

Incorporating Writing Exercises

Writing makes people think, and most people can use practice in writing, so writing exercises are clearly valuable. For example, having the learner rewrite a poorly worded workplace regulation helps the learner to achieve the learning objective of knowing the regulation, as well as enhancing writing skills. Writing provides variety and a change of pace, too. It isn't necessary for learners to write essays or novels, but short assignments are helpful. Writing blogs and sending text messages requires exactly the same skills as the writing described here.

Here are four exercises that require writing:

1. *Definitions.* When you are introducing a new subject, have learners write their definition (or their concept, perception, or whatever is appropriate) before you provide the information. For example, if you're about to introduce the concept of environmental scanning for a training course on marketing planning, have learners write their definitions of what they think (or know) it is. Review their responses before explaining the textbook definition. Often you'll find that the ones they wrote were good.

2. *Expectations.* At the beginning of a training session, have learners put down on paper (either 8½-by-11-inch sheet or newsprint for posting on the wall) what they expect to gain. Refer back to these expectations from time to time, and for sure at the end. Probe to see where there might be holes in the training, as well as to determine what extra benefits the learners might have derived from their experience. This can also be turned into a blog exercise where appropriate.

3. *Spontaneous Ideas.* Have s sheet of newsprint available for participants to jot down questions that come up, new ideas, or topics they think might be appropriate for future sessions. Review these lists periodically, because some of the items might be useful to include in the current session, perhaps at the end.

4. *Summaries.* Many segments of training end with a summary provided by the facilitator, or possibly by learners, of what was just learned. Summarizing is good management practice, and training certainly gains from it. One option is to have individual learners or groups write executive summaries of what was just covered. This doubles as a way to review material. If learners know at the

beginning that they'll be doing this, they'll start giving it thought at that time, which is exactly what you want.

 Note: These same concepts can be incorporated into e-learning materials.

Many variations stem from these four exercises, and it's a good idea to assign additional activities that require writing short pieces between training sessions. What people write on a piece of paper or key into a computer is their intellectual property. It reinforces the learning process positively, so use this technique as much as possible in training.

Making Learning Contracts

When people contract to provide a service, meet a deadline, or otherwise commit themselves to keep a promise, they tend to fulfill that commitment. This holds true in training. Learning contracts can be a matter of having learners jot down on a piece of paper (or enter on a blog, in an e-mail, or in a text message) what they intend to achieve during a training session and then keep the entry for their own use, or it can go so far as to specify precisely what skills or knowledge the learner expects to acquire, and at what level, recorded as a formal contract completed and signed in the presence of the trainer. Often, the simple versions are all that are needed to help keep learners focused on achieving learning objectives. Have learners jot down three things they expect to achieve from the training session, or perhaps what they expect to take back to their workplace that will contribute to a higher level of personal effectiveness. If practice is involved, the contract might include a statement of how they intend to keep current. Contracts can be used for any type of training, classroom or remote. For e-learning, they may be helpful in keeping individual learners on track.

Using Instruments to Learn More About Learners

The more you know about learners, the more directed your learning can become. For example, if results of completing a learning style instrument have shown that several members of the learning group are hands-on learners, they could be selected to perform demonstrations or participate in role plays, or perhaps additional exercises could be scheduled. If an organization instrument has determined that a work group undergoing training for implementing work teams is not ready to move directly into teams, the training can be altered to accommodate that fact—perhaps by including a module where the learners interview other workers to determine their level of teamwork inclination and develop a process to start changing people to accept teams.

Simply completing an instrument before, during, or after training gets the learner involved in the process, and the more involvement, the more ownership the learner will take in the overall learning process. This is particularly true when an instrument has provided information the learner can use in some way.

Holding Individual Meetings

Sometimes you need to work one-on-one with a learner. Perhaps you want to give positive feedback to a person who doesn't like to be singled out in front of the group, or perhaps you're faced with problem situations where you have to go head-to-head with the person. Some facilitators make it a point to meet with each individual at some time during the training session. This is an excellent procedure (though time consuming) that sends a message to the learner that you care and are concerned about his or her learning. For large groups, it's good practice at least to meet with those whom you notice are having problems or causing problems because, again, it shows you care about the learning that takes place. Individual meetings can also be held remotely, using appropriate technology as available.

Using Real-Time or Action Learning

The more realistic training is, the more effective it will be. This logic fits right in with adult learning theory, which tells us that adults relate learning to what they already know. Some training, of course, is automatically related directly to the workplace. For example, learning how to use a graphic presentation software package is directly related to the workplace for a person who must make such presentations as a part of the job. But if the sample situations used in the class are ones that the person will actually use (e.g., diversity, management skills), this degree of realism makes the training all the more effective.

Action learning (identified in Step Three) is training that has a real-time scenario as its basis. In other words, this training gives learners an actual workplace problem to solve. It's often done in teams that include a diverse group of learners (e.g., middle managers from a variety of plants); they are assigned the problem, and the facilitator assesses their solution. Assessment can range from critique to using the solution and grading it as if in a real performance review.

Following are some examples of how to apply real-time learning techniques:

- *Management Development Training.* Assign the group the task of developing a strategic plan for implementing a new product line. The group members, who are being groomed for higher-level positions, then have a prescribed amount of time to develop the strategic plan. They are provided with complete instructions, including any instructional material on how to develop such plans. Part of the assignment might be for the team to determine what resources and information it needs and then to find them. Upon completion of the task, the plan is reviewed and subjected to a formal critique by top management.

- *Problem-Solving Training.* Assign the group the task of developing a solution to a specific company (or departmental) problem, such as a conflict between the design group and the marketing group on how to package a product that is being updated. Perhaps marketing does not believe that its retail customers want the product tied to another product that needs to have its sales bolstered. The task could include a process whereby a review committee from both groups reviews the proposed solution and decides whether to implement it.

- *Creativity Training.* For a training course in creativity and innovation for a high-tech software company, the task for the learners could be to use a variety of creative techniques, introduced at the beginning of the course, to come up with ideas for new entertainment applications packages for consumers. Competing groups come up with their ideas, which are studied by the executive committee, with the best ones selected for development.

- *Presentation Skills Training.* The training might start with several conventional classroom sessions to learn the basics of making good presentations. Individuals are assigned the task of developing a presentation they were already scheduled to make to their departments or other work groups (e.g., a learner from the marketing group might use the requirement to give a quarterly report on new promotion campaigns and make this the basis of the presentation developed for the class). Members of the session then critique each other's presentations.

Online Learning Involvement

The act of manipulating a keyboard and mouse make e-learning literally hands-on learning. The learner must be physically and mentally engaged in the process. If the graphics, exercises, tests, and the like are well designed and presented, the learner will be stimulated—motivation will be built into the training.

Thanks to technology that makes online learning convenient and efficient, there are several ways you can get learners involved, even though you aren't on the scene. These innovations include:

- Automatic feedback at regular intervals that keeps the learner's interest high as he or she sees that progress is being made (e.g., questions that must be answered or multiple-choice selections that determine how well the learner is actually learning).
- Blogs, where learners can express their thoughts, pose questions, and otherwise communicate with others who are taking the same training.
- Text messaging, which allows everyone involved in the training to communicate with other trainees at any time the need arises. It allows communication to occur immediately, since the message comes to the receiver's cell phone or other portable device.
- Teleconferencing, which can be used as an adjunct to online learning when you need to get all learners together on occasion.
- E-mail, which works much the same as text messaging.

Some training situations call for using social Web sites to extend the training and bring learners together in a virtual world.

Step Seven

Get Feedback

> *"A world with learning and support delivered online and at work via PDAs, streaming videos, mobile phones, online knowledge bases, wikis, blogs, classrooms, communities and workplace coaching demands new inquisitiveness."*
>
> —Allison Rossett, *Training Trends*, January 2009

The sale isn't complete until the customer has paid in full. This is what sales representatives are taught. It's a solid principle that's been around a long time because it's true. The sale has to stick. The same principle applies to training (even short training sessions), because training isn't completed until performance is improved—and it's evaluation that brings the closure we need to make that determination. Success means that learners have increased their skills, which in turn increases organization effectiveness. Using a management analogy, continuous improvement applies as much to training as to manufacturing and other business processes.

Conduct evaluation not only after training is completed but during the process as well. Continual evaluation will greatly reduce the chance that your efforts ultimately will be ineffective. On a more positive note, good training can be turned into superb training if there are checkpoints along the way to determine how things are going and that allow the trainer to make proper adjustments.

If you followed Steps Two, Three, and Four carefully, you will have already done all the work of preparing for training evaluation.

American Management Association
www.amanet.org

Now, in Step Seven, you actually conduct the evaluation. (Of course, you can briefly evaluate and make improvements prior to completion of training; nonetheless, it's after the fact of a training course that you can determine ultimate results.)

Step Seven Summary

This step is closely related to learning objectives, which anchor the process of training. In addition, the concern is whether a person can perform better on the job (and more than pay back the cost of training), handle stress better (and thus reduce lost work time), behave in a nonharassing manner (and avoid embarrassing and costly investigations), or perform whatever the expected outcome of the training session was. Specific elements of this step include:

- Linking training to the previous steps
- Determining what in particular is to be evaluated
- Determining whether to evaluate and to what degree
- Identifying evaluation tools useful in training
- Taking into account time considerations (whether short- or long-term results should be evaluated, or both)

Putting Objectives to the Test

Learning objectives are the heart of training, and, directly or indirectly, they're the focus of evaluation. They were defined, in clear, measurable terms, in Step Two. They were tied to learning principles in Step Three and built into the training process during Step Four:

- *How Objectives Relate to Step Two.* A number of possible indicators of the need for training were identified in Step Two. This step starts laying out a road map for training to follow. Accordingly, Step Two provides the raw input to Step Three, so it is critical in the overall process.
- *How Objectives Relate to Step Three.* How to apply adult learning principles and deliver training in a variety of ways were addressed in Step Three. Also discussed were the concepts of core competency and mastery. Evaluation is made much easier when

the appropriate methods are built into the training, because the trainer can then deal directly with whether skills or knowledge increased. Also, knowledge, skills, and attitude objectives may require different methods of evaluation. Evaluation helps determine if the core competencies and masteries of the organization are being achieved.

- *How Objectives Relate to Step Four.* One of the elements of designing training is to identify evaluation methods to use. Once this is done, the actual tools to evaluate are developed, ready to go with the training, with learning objectives providing the substance of training.

Together these three steps prepare you to evaluate and they clearly illustrate why a total systems approach to training pays off. Exhibit 7-1 shows the direct relationship between learning objectives and evaluation; it takes sample objectives identified in Exhibit 2-5 and shows how they can be evaluated.

Determining What to Measure

There are three distinct aspects of training to measure: training results, effectiveness of the process itself, and performance of the facilitator. All are important, but the single most important is training results. Always do this, even if you merely ask a pertinent question at the end of a half-hour session. Other types of evaluation assist you in improving the process and your facilitation skills, leading to a greater likelihood that you will achieve the desired results.

Results of the Training

The first question to ask on completion of a training session is: Was the training effective? More specifically, you may need to determine if learner skills or knowledge increased or improved as designed and expected (e.g., by evaluating the learner's presentation skills) or perhaps to discover whether the desired behaviors are being practiced after the fact (e.g., by observing a person on the job to determine if he or she demonstrates greater acceptance of diversity in the workplace). Training for which the results are left to speculation or guesswork is virtually the same as ineffective training (which it may well have been), because no one will know if the learners gained new skills.

Exhibit 7-1. Sample learning objectives and appropriate tests.

Learning Objective	Appropriate Test
• State the five major phases of a Six Sigma program (performance) verbatim (standard) from memory (condition).	Written essay
• After reading a case study (condition) illustrating a Six Sigma program implementation, identify which actions were taken in each of the steps (performance), with no mistakes (standard).	Written
• Demonstrate the correct technique for performing CPR (performance), using a mannequin (condition) for five minutes (standard).	Exercise
• Type sixty-five words per minute (performance) without any mistakes (standard), using a regular PC keyboard (condition).	Demonstration
• Develop three satisfactory learning objectives for the introductory module of a stress management training course (performance), using The First-Time Trainer (condition), in thirty minutes (standard).	Written
• Parallel park a four-door sedan within the lines of a parking space (performance) during peak traffic (condition), within three minutes and having to back up no more than three times (standard).	Demonstration
• Demonstrate the proper response to an improper sexual advance (performance) during a role play (condition) in a manner acceptable to company policy (standard).	Role, demonstration, exercise
• Shut down the assembly line (performance) during a simulated equipment malfunction (condition) within five seconds after the alarm sounds (standard).	Simulation, actual equipment
• Generate a budget for the planning department (performance) that meets the company's standard budget submission requirements (standard), using a spreadsheet application program (condition).	Written, computer
• After viewing a video clip (condition), diagnose potential Americans with Disabilities	

Act violations (performance) and categorize the level of severity of each using the company policy guidelines (standard).	Oral, written

Ways to evaluate whether learning objectives were achieved can be categorized into four general types: exercises, tests of various types, questioning techniques, and post-training.

Exercises

Exercises can be used in a number of ways to evaluate training. Performance tests can be helpful in evaluating training results and work well for measuring skill-related learning objectives. The closer the tasks on the test are to actual workplace conditions, the better. If possible, conduct them as if they were part of the learner's regular work.

The purpose of this evaluation is to see if the learner can perform a task using desired skills, applying knowledge, or exhibiting desired behaviors. For example, you could have the learner compose a business letter after completing a basic word-processing training program, prepare a sample strategic plan after completing a management development program on planning, or isolate and repair a faulty circuit board using the skills just learned in a technician training program. A behavioral example is used to determine whether a person has adopted healthier habits and lifestyle, as exhibited in a role play, at the end of a stress management course.

As you can see, performance tests can take many forms. What matters is finding out whether learning objectives were met. Properly defined learning objectives often state what the test should be.

Group exercises, such as those described in Step Six, can also be used to evaluate training. They offer the advantage of not only reinforcing learning but also measuring it. They're particularly useful for measuring team training-related objectives. Trainers can use them during the training session to measure progress and at the end to measure final performance of learning objectives.

Tests

When we think of tests, we usually think back to our school days and those paper-and-pencil (or online) challenges we might well like to forget. For training, tests may be the optimum way to measure training results, particularly for knowledge-related objectives. If the learning objective is to be able to identify ten key steps to a quality assurance program (the subject of the course), you can have learners write them down, possibly with examples, to let you accurately evaluate the training results. This type of test can be classified as a knowledge test (rather than a skills test). There are other types of tests, as well:

- *Binary Choice.* The answers to these are right or wrong, true or false. Use these sparingly unless you have used them orally during training. The answer must be clearly right; avoid trick questions.
- *Multiple Choice.* These help you determine whether learners have retained the desired knowledge and can weed out unimportant information. Be sure there is just one clear answer, and be careful about terminology and jargon. It's important that only one answer is clearly the correct one, no matter how close to being correct the others are. Otherwise it is an unfair question.
- *Matching.* These are similar to multiple choice. Use them to determine whether learners are acquiring specific terminology and relationships. Be careful about terminology and jargon. Certain terms are important parts of the learning process, but they must have been made known to the learner in advance.
- *Completion.* Again, this is similar to both matching and multiple-choice tests. Answers need to be clear to avoid confusion.
- *Essay.* Essays are good for behavior and manager- and executive-related training. You should have predetermined key points that the trainees should make in their written answers. Don't leave the essay too open-ended unless it's a creative assignment.

Evaluating tests gets more difficult as you go down the line from, say, a true-or-false test to a test in which the trainees evaluate a case study and answer in essay form.

Tests can take many forms. For short sessions or for an interim evaluation, oral tests work well and simplify the process. Written tests require preparation time but are easy to maintain through word processors. Having learners take tests directly on a personal computer system also works if it is within the scope of the training to develop computer skills. Standard tests can also be used. Be careful not to ask trick or ambiguous questions, and also be aware that some cultures have difficulty with negatively phrased questions on tests.

Online learning software generally includes a testing capability, so these considerations apply equally to this type of learning.

How can you determine if a test is right for a situation? Exhibit 7-2 asks questions that will help you decide.

Exhibit 7-2. To test or not to test: A dozen questions to help you decide.

1. Is there a faster way to obtain feedback?
2. Does the learner have to perform the task or tasks right away afer returning to the job?
3. Is safety involved?
4. Would failure to meet the objective(s) be costly to the organization?
5. Is the element under consideration a basic requirement before the trainee can go on to a more vital element (i.e., a key building block for further objectives)?
6. Was enough knowledge provided for the learner to be properly tested?
7. Will the learner most likely do well on the test?
8. Are there clear-cut answers to the test?
9. If there are no clear-cut answers (e.g., a test on complex ethics issues), can you defend the answers you expect as a facilitator?
10. Is there an easier way to obtain feedback?
11. Does the learning objective lend itself to testing (rather than having the trainee actually perform the objective)?
12. Will the test measure it accurately?

If you answered no to either question 1 or 10 and yes to any of the other questions, testing could be of value. Another consideration is whether there is enough time to prepare, deliver, and grade the test, regardless of what type it is.

Questioning Techniques

Questions are excellent for measuring knowledge-related objectives. Refer to the Step Six discussion on asking questions.

Exhibit 7-3. Sample training evaluation form.

Training Session: _____

Facilitator: _____ Date: _____

For each item below, check the line under the number you believe best applies, using the criteria: 1 = strongly disagree; 2 = disagree, 3 = not sure, 4 = agree, 5 = strongly agree

Item	1	2	3	4	5
1. I will be able to use these skills (knowledge) on my job.	___	___	___	___	___
2. Learning objectives were clear.	___	___	___	___	___
3. I could easily relate to examples and problems used.	___	___	___	___	___
4. Subject matter was presented in an orderly manner.	___	___	___	___	___
5. The facilitator was well prepared.	___	___	___	___	___
6. The facilitator was knowledgeable in the subject matter.	___	___	___	___	___
7. The facilitator paid close attention to learner needs and questions.	___	___	___	___	___
8. The materials were useful.	___	___	___	___	___
9. The audiovisuals added to the session.	___	___	___	___	___
10. The training length was just about right.	___	___	___	___	___
11. I would recommend this training to others.	___	___	___	___	___

Your comments are appreciated for future improvements, so please add anything else you feel is pertinent, including any changes you recommend. _____
_____
_____
_____
_____

Thank you for taking time to complete this evaluation!

Posttraining

One of the best ways to evaluate training is to follow up on learners after they have returned to work. Although this is one of the best means of follow-up, it is probably the least practiced because it requires time and resources. A reasonable assumption is that a learner's supervisor can tell if the person's performance has improved. The supervisor was likely involved in selecting the learner for training, meaning that the supervisor has a vested interest in the training outcome. It is logical, then, to ask the supervisor how well the training worked. Did the learner perform better after returning to the workplace or become more productive?

Typically, follow-up surveys are conducted at defined points after the training and can be done more than once. For instance, following up three months after training may allow enough time to determine what level of improvement took place. Sometimes it's appropriate to wait six months or even longer. If the training was a lengthy oral and written communications improvement course, it may take months to determine the ultimate effectiveness.

Follow-up surveys can be conducted by telephone, through formal, written forms, online, or by e-mail. Considering that the real test of training effectiveness is on-the-job performance, surveying supervisors is more valuable than performance tests conducted during and immediately after training.

Evaluating the Training Process

Implementing the theme of continuous improvement requires that all aspects of the training process, including the actual process of delivering training, be evaluated. There are several ways to accomplish this evaluation:

1. *Self-Assessment by the Facilitator.* A competent facilitator can give a good indication of results, providing that assessment is done objectively.
2. *A Survey of Participants.* The learners have a sense of how well the training went and may have ideas for improving future applications. Exhibit 7-3 shows a sample form for learner feedback.

3. *Outside Observers.* This may cost more, but, done properly, it can have a positive effect on future training done by the facilitator.

4. *Videotape.* Videotaping sessions provides a relatively true picture of what transpired. There's nothing quite like listening and watching oneself perform. This technique can show many details that the facilitator was not aware of.

5. *Review of Performance Test Results.* This is the ultimate test. If learners can meet desired objectives, then the facilitator did the job.

Using combinations of these may be more effective than applying just one.

Facilitator Performance

The purposes of this type of evaluation are to determine if you were as effective as possible in delivering training and, more important, to help you improve your facilitation efforts. Key focal points include application of adult learning concepts, extensive learner involvement, effective use of time, and evidence that learning objectives were achieved.

Facilitator performance evaluations can be accomplished in two ways. The first is *self-evaluation,* as noted earlier. Self-evaluation is an integral part of continuous improvement, since it includes trainer performance, as well. You can use the evaluation form shown in Exhibit 7-3, possibly adding a few key items of interest to you. The example given is appropriate for a classroom training session, but, with a few changes, it can easily be adapted for an online delivered course. *All* training must be evaluated, no matter how it was delivered.

The second way to evaluate facilitator performance is *learner evaluation,* also noted earlier. If learners are considered to be competent adults who want to learn and acquire new skills, then it stands to reason they'll have a good idea of whether the training was successful and how well it was delivered. Many learners have attended numerous training sessions and perhaps have conducted training themselves. This experience gives them an excellent yardstick with which to assess trainer performance. (Again refer to the sample evaluation form shown in Exhibit 7-3.)

When and How Much to Evaluate

Since time is always of the essence—there is *never* enough of it to exhaust every aspect of each step in the training process—you are challenged to determine how much evaluation is enough. Here are some thoughts to bear in mind when designing training and paying heed to the critical evaluation element:

1. Build as much evaluation into the process as possible, which will render after-the-fact evaluation (other than that done later, on the job) much less important. Several performance measurements during training will serve quite well and take far less time than testing participants when the training is done.

2. Prioritize evaluation according to how critical the training is to meeting the organization's objectives. If the company's competitiveness depends on the training (e.g., if training is related to shifting to a new product base and marketing it in an international arena), then evaluation is mandatory.

3. Identify evaluation methods during Step Four so that evaluation after training can be accomplished relatively quickly.

Software Evaluation Tools

New tools for the trainer to use continue to be developed and implemented. One is the so-called learning management system. It's safe to say there is software for just about anything you might want to do with training (provided you have the equipment and the staff to use it), and it may or may not be appropriate for you. Some packages cover the full spectrum of the training process: signing up learners for the training, delivering the training, tracking learners' progress, and finally assisting in evaluating learner outcomes. If you don't have experience in these or similar systems, it's advisable to seek advice on what to use as well as on how to use it.

See Step Eight and Resources for ways you can learn more.

Step Eight

Improve Continuously

> *"Put your ears to the tracks, and you'll hear the rumbling of a freight train coming toward you. It's Web 2.0, and it's driven by the sounds of millions of conversations across the blogosphere, the growing hum of business podcasts, and the steady accretion of institutional wisdom on corporate wikis."*
>
> —Anders Gronstedt, *T+D*, December 2008

Successful trainers never stop learning and growing. Technology, changes in the workplace, and global competition are three prime reasons that it's essential for you to keep up with new developments. In recognition of this professional need, Step Eight addresses the vital element of professional development.

If you're a one-time trainer, you *can* ignore this step. Still, there are a few things you might want to consider to help make your training sessions the best they can be. If you'll be training regularly, the advice given in this step will help you fulfill your quest for stretching and improving your own performance. There's another consideration worth thinking about: Anticipation (such as in a learning organization) can lead a company to provide vital training before a problem indicates the need for it. Everyone in the workplace, and certainly anyone who is a manager, is concerned with skills enhancement and competency. Thinking like a trainer and staying on top of things will serve you well on the job.

Step Eight Summary

Professionalism as a trainer encompasses many facets. Primary ones discussed in this step are:

- Review of the skills trainers need
- Ways to enhance these skills
- The portfolio concept for managing and maintaining skills
- Technology and the need for trainers to keep up with what's available
- Trainer's ethics
- Summary of the eight steps to effective training

Training Skills Revisited

Step One identified a number of skills that trainers need (actually, they are closely related to the skills all knowledge workers need). The purpose of professional development is to improve these skills, as well as to take steps to acquire any newly emerging skills. As a review, here are those skills:

- *Management Skills.* To ensure success within tight budgets. A trainer manages time (including time for learners who are away from their jobs for training), resources, and funds, as well as training staff members.
- *Communication Skills.* To motivate, among other goals.
- *Analytical and Problem-Solving Skills.* To tackle needs assessment and more.
- *Information Literacy.* To find information and implement solutions to problems.
- *Computer Literacy.* To gain access to information accessible only by computer. Additionally, computers are often essential for performing on the job; communications rely on automation, and computers have become a prime method of delivering training.

Professional development should be based on a review of these skills. Starting with an inventory of where you stand on each one, you can lay out a plan to focus on the ones that need the most work.

These skills will form headings under your portfolio, discussed later in this step.

Strengthening Training Skills

There are numerous ways to stay up-to-date as a trainer. It may be a simple matter of finding an article on a particular aspect of training, or, on a broader note, affiliating and networking with a professional association. We examine a number of ways here to strengthen skills.

Speaking and Training Opportunities

Many opportunities exist for maintaining your speaking and training skills. One available in many locations is Toastmasters. Here you'll have the chance to hone your ability to stand before a group and speak and to receive valuable feedback. Many volunteer opportunities exist, as well. The value is that these opportunities allow you to sharpen the public-speaking skills that are essential for most training situations, particularly when the instructor is central to the process, as in classroom training. These skills are also the topic of training in many organizations, since so many people need to improve them. When you think about all the volunteer organizations there are, and how much training they have to offer (e.g., Scouting, senior centers, rehabilitation programs, youth sports, YMCA and YWCA, adult learning centers), you quickly realize how much opportunity there is for you to give talks and improve your public-speaking skills, as well as provide much-needed training for these organizations. Also, service clubs—and there are many of them—seek to put on as many as fifty programs a year, providing enormous opportunity for speaking and training.

There are also opportunities related to e-learning and computer-based training. Developing and developing automated training courses for the types of organizations mentioned in the previous paragraph, rather than for classroom delivery, provide opportunities to add to your training skills. No question about it: The more experience you have, the better able you are to become a professional trainer with advanced skills.

A proven way to gain skills as a trainer is to be a learner yourself. You can improve your own training skills (as well as other appropriate workplace skills), while being exposed to many types of training delivered in many different ways. The more you do this, the better you'll become at quickly recognizing which training is effective and which is not.

Professional Associations

The primary national training organization, the American Society for Training and Development (ASTD), provides extensive services for trainers, from beginners to senior-level professionals. Most major cities have chapters, and you can be a member of the national or the local organization or both. Local chapters offer services including special-interest groups, professional development, a wide variety of online options, workshops, and meetings. You can contact the national ASTD at www.astd.org; 703-683-8100 voice; 703-683-8103 fax; or 1640 King St., Alexandria, VA 22313. Local chapter information can be accessed from the national Web site. ASTD provides publications, chat groups, networking opportunities, databases, a job bank, and much more.

Becoming an ASTD member is unquestionably one of the best things a trainer can do. Not only will you be in a position to become more professional and accomplished as a trainer, but you'll also have a wealth of resources available at your fingertips (see Appendix A on resources).

Many other training-related organizations exist, but generally they are geared to specialists in various applications, such as organization development. Check with a local library or through Internet sources for assistance and information on resources. In fact, the Internet and the World Wide Web can provide you with a significant portion of what you need for professional development—which is no surprise considering the level of their use in everyday training.

Publications

Vast numbers of professional publications are available for trainers, both online and in print. Most major publishers of business- and workplace-related materials publish in the training field. Two magazines of interest to all trainers—first-time and experienced—are *Training Magazine* and *T + D* (published by ASTD). Both are available in print and online versions. For *T + D*, use the ASTD contact information previously given. *Training* can be reached at www. trainingmag.com. Both regularly contain current information on developments in the training and development field and are useful for information regarding specific training questions. A search through the index of these two magazines will lead you to valuable information. The amount of information available online is more than enough to keep trainers updated.

Commercial Sources

An enormous supply of materials is commercially available: workshops and seminars, certificate and degree programs, games and simulations, experiential materials, instruments, handbooks, and other materials. If you search for training and development books on a book provider's Web site, you'll find plenty of books on the subjects, with detailed information about what's in them. Professional development tools, as well as off-the-shelf materials on numerous training topics, are marketed that may fill your training need. Contract trainers and consultants are widely available. These resources can be reached through the two magazines already mentioned, through ASTD, electronically, and through local contacts, as well as through Web sites and the Yellow Pages. Training is a big business, so you don't have to go far to locate most of the resources you'll need.

The Trainer's Portfolio

Professionals have long used portfolios to exhibit their skills and accomplishments. The concept is adaptable to any career and offers an effective way of presenting personal skills and qualifications. You'll still need a résumé, but it should merely reflect your current qualifications for a particular position or field (i.e., a summation of your portfolio). Otherwise, it's typically too broad to merit consideration from the hiring (or contracting) body. The idea is to keep adding to your portfolio—it needs to be updated on a regular basis. Maintaining a portfolio is an excellent way for part-time trainers to keep up with this field.

Your own portfolio (valid for both training opportunities and your profession) might contain these categories (as well as others that fit your individual needs):

- Professional development
- New skills within the industry or profession (e.g., use of the workplace and trainer skills identified in Step One: information literacy, interpersonal communication problem solving and decision making, and creativity and innovation)
- Computer and other technology skills, including software application packages you are qualified in
- Interpersonal skills (communication, writing, motivation)
- Education—formal degree programs, certificate programs, workshops, and seminars
- Community and professional service (volunteering), which themselves might be subdivided into the categories already listed
- Other skills that are transferable to other jobs or professions (e.g., total quality management, diversity expertise, team development experience)
- Outside interests, to show you as a whole person (e.g., recreation, fitness and wellness, vocational interests)

There are plenty of opportunities to acquire skills and experiences outside the job itself, including:

- Volunteering
- Tutoring
- Religious organizations
- Industry associations
- Writing
- Workshops and conferences
- Certificate programs
- Temporary firm training
- Professional mail (from associations)
- Internet searches
- Informational interviews
- Nonprofit agencies
- Toastmasters
- Mentoring (and being mentored)
- Professional associations

- Reading
- Internships (paying and nonpaying)
- Observation
- Degree programs
- Speakers' bureaus
- Adult education programs
- Coaching (and being coached)
- Networking

A note about networking: This is facilitated through electronic means of communication and should be pursued to the greatest extent possible.

Technology and Training

Technology has become a driver of training in most organizations. There are two reasons for this: Organizations must have the latest technology in order to remain competitive (even the nonprofit ones); and technology provides a highly effective way to design, prepare, deliver, and evaluate training. Technology changes rapidly. The challenge for you, the trainer, is to stay on top of what is coming, what may come down the line, and how you and your organization can take advantage of it. And don't forget, classroom training, training's old standby, is very much alive and well.

Technology Scanning

Among the best ways to keep up with new developments are following the technology news, reading blogs by experts, and listening to your friends and colleagues. This will keep you apprised of anything that may be of use to your training efforts. After a while, you will have a good knowledge of where to get the best information. Web searches can yield plenty of information if you use patience and carefully screen the sites. Many sites allow you to observe a sample run of a program. The wide range of training delivery systems—from classroom to remote Internet access—provides you with plenty of options and proves that the old and the new go together quite well.

A Word About Ethics

Concern about ethics within the realm of training falls into two categories: being ethical in facilitating the learning process and in delivering ethics-related training. There is no question about the need to be concerned about ethics in the workplace. Just reading the latest business news to see who tried to bilk companies, customers, or organizations out of enormous sums of money is proof enough. From the training viewpoint, ethics is a matter of being fair in all dealings with others, including ensuring that every participant in a training session receives the best support and facilitation you can offer. It also means expecting participants to be ethical.

Conducting ethics training is easy to do (perhaps too easy—making it a matter of merely paying lip service). There's plenty of material—videos, cases, books, exercises—on the market, and many organizations are paying attention to it, some because they want to, others because they have to. The material is uncomplicated and can be easily grasped by participants.

There's another aspect of ethics. Automated workplace systems make it easy to attach sensors and other software to gather data about workers. This can be quite useful for needs assessment, as well as evaluating training. But a word of caution: Make sure there is no question about invasion of privacy when such sensors are used.

Here are some thoughts to keep in mind if you find yourself concerned about ethics from a training viewpoint:

- Base everything you do, from actions to ethics training programs, on your organization's values statement.
- Don't pass judgment on others, particularly participants.
- Use examples that members of your training group can easily relate to.
- Practice what you preach.
- Don't portray cases and people in ways that aren't true to life in your organization (unless for discussion or contrasting purposes).

Eight Steps to Effective Training: A Summary

Effective training is as easy as taking the eight steps identified in this book. Of course, it is rarely easy to do anything well, and training requires a lot of hard, but satisfying, work. The idea is that if you follow a series of steps, you increase the chance that training will be effective. The eight steps, summarized in Exhibit 8-1, also serve as focal points for continuous improvement. Exhibit 8-2 notes some of the things that can be done to improve each of the steps.

Exhibit 8-1. Eight steps to effective training.

1. *Facilitate learning*—This element is the key to trainer success and includes how to implement the other seven steps. The trainer facilitates the process, depending on a well-designed program and motivated learners for the training to be effective.
2. *Focus on performance*—Establish the objective of the training and make sure you're on track—*before* you start. Objectives are derived from needs assessment, both of which must be done before attempting to do any meaningful training.
3. *Focus on learning*—Make sure the training provides the maximum possibility for participant learning, with emphasis on how adults and organizations learn. Using adult learning principles and a focus on mastery and competence will ensure the best training possible.
4. *Be prepared*—Develop the materials you'll need, bringing them all together in the most effective order, and making sure everything is ready to go. There are many things to do and many options (media, delivery methods, learners, trainers, evaluation methods). Thanks to a dedicated profession, there are plenty of tools and techniques to help get these important tasks done.
5. *Deliver effectively*—Develop the communication skills you'll need to present your training session successfully. Even if the training is fully automated or otherwise requires little trainer intervention, communication is critical. Online training requires that the training package be carefully communicated to the training technicians who are producing it.
6. *Get learners involved*—Develop the best in all participants, and practice different ways to deliver the training. This step is tied closely to the previous steps. Thanks to trainers who take the profession seriously, there are a number of field-tested ways to do this.

7. **Get feedback**—Determine the success of the training. Evaluation should occur all through the training process, and particularly when it's over. It's the only way you'll know if desired learning objectives are being met.

8. **Improve continuously**—Keep your trainer's portfolio up-to-date and enhance your skills as a trainer.

Exhibit 8-2. Ways to increase professionalism in the eight steps.

1. **Facilitate learning.** The more confidence you have as a trainer, the easier it is to think of yourself as a facilitator. At all times, keep reminding yourself that your purpose in life as a trainer is to facilitate. Try serving in a facilitator role in other things you do. All the skills identified in this step help develop facilitation skills.

2. **Focus on performance.** If you're adept at identifying learning objectives or at least are competent in recognizing them and capable of delivering training that helps learners achieve them, then you'll have focused on performance. Another way to enhance your professionalism in this regard is to think in terms of the bottom line of the training. Profit, productivity, service, or some other output must be made more effective if the training is successful. Your bottom line must coincide with that of your organization's.

3. **Focus on learning.** Becoming fully conversant with adult learning principles and adopting the concept of the learning organization (see Step One) will help you keep the focus on learning.

4. **Be prepared.** This requires diligence, patience, and much hard work. By exhibiting more of each of these three qualities, you will be better prepared.

5. **Deliver effectively.** Constant attention, including attending communication training yourself, will increase your delivery skills.

6. **Get learners involved.** This requires paying constant attention to the process, including always being on the lookout for new exercises and ideas.

7. **Get feedback.** Ask questions constantly and apply what you learn to improve for next time.

8. **Improve continuously.** As stated in Step 8.

Trainers are always looking for checklists. Good ones provide a concise, handy, and professional tool for being competent as a trainer.

As a summary, a trainer's dozen items—points for a good trainer to keep in mind and apply—are listed in Exhibit 8-3. Apply all of them, and you'll be an effective trainer.

Exhibit 8-3. A trainer's dozen.

Here is an eclectic list of points to remember to help you become—and remain—an effective trainer:

1. Your customer is the learner. The learner replaces the sun (and everything else) as the center of your universe.
2. The trainer who can't do a passable job working somewhere within the line operations of the organization being served is suspect.
3. Technology—hard, soft, and otherwise—is nothing more than a tool. Use it as much as possible, provided that you know its effect on people. If a particular technology can make things better or more effective, use it; otherwise, wait for something better to come along. Remember, it's the person (trainer) who causes the technology to achieve training objectives.
4. The trainer who stops learning is a retired trainer.
5. Things can always get better—and it's your job to make them so.
6. Practice what you preach—by coaching, mentoring, managing, and growing. Otherwise, turn in your pointers and remote devices and become a politician.
7. To be truly professional, remember the three R's: reading, 'riting, and return on investment.
8. Paper your walls with things like the Scout's motto and the Golden Rule. Then read your walls daily.
9. Read the funny papers, go to the movies, take a hike, or go bird-watching regularly—and practice the principle of transfer of training. There's nothing more refreshing than a trainer who can relate the training situation to the bigger picture of life.
10. Remember that you can be replaced.
11. When all else fails, call ASTD, Dear Abby, SPCA, your shrink, or another practitioner like yourself. There's always professional help available.
12. Unlike in total quality assurance programs (where every step must be 100 percent successful), coming out ahead on seven or eight points out of twelve isn't bad.

Appendix A

Resources for the First-Time Trainer

Trainers don't just train—they stay busy contributing valuable resources to the profession they practice. It's all part of what they are—a truly professional group that contributes to the bottom line of the organizations they serve. They write, blog, mentor, and provide assistance to all the others who follow them. The result is an ever-growing list of books, articles, online materials, scripts for audio and video programs, instruments, reports, software applications, and more. This wealth of materials comes in many forms, from words on paper to exotic multimedia-based programs—and a growing quantity of online materials. It's interesting that new technologies and forms of resources supplement but do not replace types of materials that have been around a long time. Thus, the old standby books still have their place alongside newer forms such as podcasts and Webcasts. The profession is loaded with materials, most of which are readily available to the first-time trainer. Step Eight, Improve Continuously, provides a rich source of training resources for trainers.

This abundance of material creates a challenge for the new trainer. There simply isn't an all-inclusive catalog you can go to if you want to find, say, a good video on performance evaluation. The closest thing to a catalog, in fact, is the Internet. Go there, call up a search engine you're comfortable with, and start searching. Major categories of training resources include publications (books and periodicals), videos, training programs, products and services, and online materials and services.

American Management Association
www.amanet.org

Because of this depth of materials, any attempt to list specific sources would be quite an arbitrary exercise. It will take you but a short while to identify a wide selection within any of the following categories of resources by doing one of these things:

- Search the ASTD Web site.
- Search the *Training* magazine site.
- Search the World Wide Web.

A Web search should include a look at online booksellers for books and related materials.

American Society for Training and Development

The American Society for Training and Development (ASTD) offers just about anything and everything a new trainer could ask for when it comes to resources. A look at the Web site alone (www.astd. org) provides this sampling: publications, including books and the informative *T+D* journal; newsletters, delivered by e-mail, on such topics as e-learning, general training news, and evaluation and return on investment; career-enhancing Webcasts; certification podcasts; YouTube videos, and a wide variety of educational programs. It's an impressive array of resources for any trainer.

Joining ASTD and logging onto the Web site immediately gives you access to the following (and more):

- Conferences
- Discussion groups
- Blogs
- Awards
- Education programs
- Publications (in-depth and in a wide variety, in many forms)
- Certification programs
- Publishing opportunities
- Online and print *T + D*
- Subscription opportunities for a variety of e-mail resources, including newsletters)
- Chapter information
- Training suppliers

- Career center
- Trainer competency model

Educational programs are available for many of the topics in this book (e.g., action, e-, and blended learning; talent management; coaching, using various programs). As indicated in Step Eight, joining this organization is to any trainer's advantage—and it will provide you with many resources that you will find useful. This is also a useful summary of what is available to you via the Internet.

You're encouraged to check out the information available on the Web site. You'll be able to see the valuable resources you can access through additional membership benefits.

Training Magazine

Training magazine offers many of the same resources as ASTD, with a subscription (online, print, or both) required to obtain the full range of resources it has to offer. These include:

- Industry guides
- Toolkit
- Industry contacts
- Events and conferences
- Publications
- Blogs
- Newsletters
- *Training* magazine
- Annual training industry survey

Note: The annual survey has long been an excellent chronicle of what types of training is being conducted, how much organizations are spending, and more—a bellwether of training trends.

Web Searches

Conduct a Web search for a particular type of training material, and you'll find a number of sophisticated Web sites provided by vendors. For example, video vendors may provide the capability for you to view a short clip of the videos they sell on the site. For software and system vendors, you'll find sample uses of the programs. All this provides you with far more information than you'd get simply by seeing the name of a video on a piece of paper or listed on a screen. You'll find all the potential books you'll need from the two sites mentioned already and from online booksellers. In short, the Internet and the World Wide Web will be your online catalog. See the list in Exhibit A-1 for possible Web search topics. As you gain more experience, you will undoubtedly add many more of your own to the list.

Exhibit A-1. Major Web search topics.

Step One: Facilitate Learning

- Terms from training types listed in Exhibit 1-1
- Interpersonal communications
- Trainer skills
- Problem solving
- Decision making
- Creativity training
- Computer literacy
- Information literacy
- Management skills
- Leadership training
- Workplace learning professionals

Step Two: Focus on Performance

- Needs assessment
- Gap analysis
- Task and skill analysis
- Focus groups
- Brainstorming
- Interviewing techniques
- Questionnaires
- Training instruments
- Learning objectives

Step Three: Focus on Learning

- Knowledge learning (also cognitive learning)
- Skills learning (also called psychomotor skills)
- Attitude learning (also called affective learning)
- Learning styles
- Adult learning theory
- Learning principles
- Multimodality
- Core competency
- Mastery
- Learning how to learn
- Action learning
- The learning organization

Step Four: Be Prepared

- Classroom training
- Computer-based training
- E-learning
- Rapid e-learning
- Asynchronous training
- Self-paced learning
- Blended training
- Training simulation
- Teleconferencing
- Training videos/DVDs
- Dry boards
- Presentation systems
- Presentation software

- Digital projectors
- Overhead projectors
- Training podcasts
- Training Webcasts
- Webinars
- Training blogs
- Training wikis
- Icebreakers
- Training games
- Team building
- Role playing
- Storyboarding

Step Five: Deliver Effectively

- Communication types listed in Exhibit 5-1
- Presentation skills
- Verbal skills
- Listening skills
- Training motivation
- Workplace diversity
- Accommodating older workers
- Baby boomer characteristics
- Generation X characteristics
- Generation Y characteristics
- Accommodating disabilities
- Humor in training

Step Six: Get Learners Involved

- Group dynamics
- Difficult group behaviors
- Questioning techniques
- Types of questions
- Experiential exercises
- Learning contracts
- Self-paced learning

Step Seven: Get Feedback

- Testing techniques
- Training evaluation
- Performance measurement

Step Eight: Improve Continuously

- Training and development associations
- Toastmasters
- Workplace ethics
- Networking techniques
- Training software
- Training vendors
- Learning management systems

A last thought: There's no better way to make training choices and decisions than to solicit advice from someone else whom you can trust. Such assistance is available both in person and electronically if you take the time to seek others out. Don't hesitate to contact a particular trainer if you see he or she has published an article on something you're interested in. Networking has long served trainers well.

Appendix B

Additional Trainer Guidelines

Trainers appreciate help. In fact, the profession is known for sharing information, characteristic of its continuing effort to enhance its professional stature. The purpose of this appendix is to expand upon selected material in the text. The text lays out the basics; this appendix adds depth to selected material, providing you with background on how particular theories and practices came into being. Use these guidelines freely as you apply your training skills, all the while building new skills and reinforcing old ones. Add your own materials and references as you progress through your training career. The guidelines are divided into the following sections:

- *Guidelines for How People Learn.* We continue to discover more about this as people learn more about how the brain functions (the brain, in fact, learning about itself).
  Applicable section: Step Three, Focus on Learning
- *Guidelines for Dealing with Multiple Generations in the Workplace.* The workplace is becoming increasingly diverse, in particular with regard to the age range of the workforce. Trainers must be aware of these differences.
  Applicable section: Step Five, Deliver Effectively
- *Guidelines for Conducting Evaluation.* Evaluation is always a challenge, yet it is needed to determine the value of training and to improve future training.
  Applicable section: Step Seven, Get Feedback

- *Guidelines for Determining Whether or not Training Is Worth the Expense.* Return on investment (ROI) is the literal and the figurative bottom line of all training.
  Applicable section: Step Seven, Get Feedback
- *Guidelines for Professional Development.* As all professional people know, we can never have too much of this. Continuous trainer improvement has a direct and positive impact on future training.
  Applicable section: Step Eight, Improve Continuously

Guidelines for How People Learn (Step Three)

There are many theories about how people learn. Two of them, Bloom's Taxonomy and Gardner's multiple intelligences, are briefly presented here to provide you with a deeper level of knowledge about how people learn. We're all different, and the more aware you are about known differences, the more effective you'll be as a trainer.

Bloom's Taxonomy

Professor Benjamin Bloom (*Taxonomy of Educational Objectives*, Addison-Wesley, 1956) identified six levels of learning, and it was from these levels that the three major types of learning were adapted (see Step Three, Focus on Learning, for details of each of these levels):

- Cognitive
- Affective
- Psychomotor

The levels are included here to provide the trainer with a broader awareness about how people learn. This material was gathered from a variety of Web sites, illustrating the ready availability of training materials. The six levels of learning are:

1. *Knowledge.* The learner can recall facts about the concept. Training learners to implement new safety rules and to implement new supply requisition procedures, for example, requires that they recall facts. A sailor can recite the rules of the nautical road. Being

able to state facts is how you prove that learning objectives were met.

2. *Comprehension.* The learner can state the meaning of the concept. Indoctrinating Marines about the meaning and ultimately the practice of "Semper Fi" requires that they know why the concept is so important. The fact is that Marine esprit de corps is essential for their performance; comprehension provides the reason why this is so important.

3. *Application.* The learner can apply the concept. Training classes to learn how to use a computer presentation system ultimately requires that the learners demonstrate that they can prepare such a presentation. As in the Marine analogy, the concept is applied when Marines hold nothing back as they support one another in carrying out a mission.

4. *Analysis.* The learner can break down the concept into its various parts. Training in decision making requires that the learners be able to perform analysis to determine if the best decision has been reached. A major objective of training in thinking skills is to help the learner analyze material.

5. *Synthesis.* The learner can integrate the newly learned concept into previously learned material. Questions asked by the facilitator during training might ask learners to determine what other skills they have that might be reinforced by the newly learned material (e.g., how they could apply creative thinking techniques to solving a product delivery problem). Synthesis is extremely important to professional and management training.

6. *Evaluation.* The learner can use the concept to make decisions. Management and executive development training falls into this category, as the intent is to prepare learners for higher level performance. It's the ultimate level of intelligence.

Note how similar these six steps are to the steps in the information literacy skill (Step One). In most cases, a trainer's goal is to achieve the highest level of learning (evaluation). When you recognize that there are several tiers that a learner must go through, you'll be better prepared to design and develop training that will most effectively lead to achieving learning objectives.

Also note how each of these types builds on the type before

it. For example, many training evolutions require that the learner acquire knowledge before moving on toward more critical learning outcomes (i.e., applying that knowledge). A challenge for the trainer is that evaluation and return on investment determination become more difficult as one goes from the knowledge level of learning to the evaluation level of learning. You will find it helpful to give thought to these levels as you acquire new trainer skills.

Gardner's Multiple Intelligences

Professor Howard Gardner of Harvard developed a theory of multiple intelligences, showing that people use a variety of senses as they function, including as they learn. His ideas are outlined in two books (*Frames of Mind* [Basic Books, 1983]) and *Intelligence Reframed* [Basic Books, 1999]), as well as in a variety of other sources. Seven of the types of intelligence identified by Gardner are noted here. Keep these in mind when you design, develop, and deliver training; doing so can help you ensure that maximum learning takes place. Not everyone fits precisely into one of these categories, and you'll realize that many of us learn in more than one way. Yet anything that can enhance training is worth considering. This is what is meant by using as much variety in training as possible (Step Three, Focus on Learning). The types of intelligence are:

- *Linguistic Intelligence.* Learners who are verbal learn best by listening to information, such as that presented in lectures and podcasts. You'll find them sitting in the front row for a lecture, buried in a book in the library, or never without earphones and a personal device at the ready. They take advantage of notes, texts, and anything else that is written. When there is something to read to learn about the subject, they are likely to learn well on their own. Most traditional training in the past has been based on learner linguistic intelligence.
- *Musical Intelligence.* These are learners who appreciate music and sounds. Where sound effects can be incorporated into the learning, learners who have a degree of music intelligence will become more apt to learn. This is one of the more obscure learning types and is less likely than others to be of advantage to the trainer.
- *Logical-Mathematical Intelligence.* Learners who use logic and reason are good at analyzing situations and are oriented toward

problem solving. They perform well in learning to sort out case studies and to comprehend large bodies of knowledge. These learners do well in various types of thinking skills training.

- *Spatial Intelligence.* Learners who are visual in their approach to learning respond well to visual aids such as pictures, drawings, and graphs. They can flow-chart concepts in the learning environment. Technical training that requires learners to see the "big picture" is an example of training that uses this learning type. Flight training relies heavily on spatial intelligence.

- *Bodily-Kinesthetic Intelligence.* Learners who are hands-on in everything they do perform well in e-learning because they are manipulating the means of learning (e.g., the mouse and the cursor). The same holds true for videoconferencing, where you are on camera and your body language can be seen. Outdoor training is based on this type of learning, as well as any training using equipment, machinery, or the like.

- *Interpersonal Intelligence.* Learners who work well with others, such as in group learning activities, do especially well in team-building exercises. Role playing is another learning method where they can excel. For e-learning, the use of various communication channels allows close, personal relationships within the online training environment even though the learner is in a virtual classroom.

- *Intrapersonal Intelligence.* These learners do well on their own, having the confidence that they can take charge of their fates and complete the learning assignment. They are good at reflecting upon their experiences and then moving on to the next level of learning. Learning where the material is completed on the learner's own time works well for this type of learner.

Two further comments:

- Pause and reflect on how you learn and how you can expand on your styles. The more you know about yourself, the more you'll know about the learners you work with.
- Use professional development time to learn more about these levels as you become a more seasoned practitioner.

Three other intelligences Gardner has identified—naturalistic, spiritual, and existential intelligence—are not covered here. The point here is not to try to classify learners into distinct categories (even if it might be possible), but simply to be aware that people learn in many different ways, and the more ways you can stimulate, the greater chance that the training's learning objectives will be met—which is all you want to do.

Guidelines for Dealing with Multiple Generations in the Workplace (Step Five)

The introduction to this book points out that people from several generations are present in the workforce, each with its own characteristics, needs, and approaches to work and life. If you know that these differences exist and what they are, you can perform far more effectively as a trainer by accommodating these needs in your training. The generations and their characteristics are:

- Older workers—born during or before World War II. Though of retirement age, you will still find many of them at work. Some have returned to the workforce, while some have never retired. They prefer to keep working, and many need the income. The reason doesn't matter—they need training as much as anyone else, and they may not be tuned into the technology applied to training. They are traditional in their values, which include having respect for authority and typically staying with the same employer throughout one's career (and they are often shocked when they are let go). They are the least technology-oriented learners the trainer will become involved with. This is a special challenge to you as a trainer. Remember, they must use technology and have the skills to do so, so be patient if it takes them longer to adapt to technology. This group grew up with traditional classroom training and no personal computers.
- Baby boomers—born between 1946 and 1964. These are the people who are causing strains on retirement systems, although many still work (for the same reason as the older colleagues). They're more up-to-date with technology but not nearly as much as the generations that have followed them. They are work oriented, feeling that they have paid their dues. They are considered independent and self-reliant, goal oriented and ready to compete. They entered the workforce during economically good

times, when the economy was shifting to service industries. They are comfortable with technology; though they started out with traditional training methods, they soon became familiar with technology-facilitated training, as well.

- Generation X—born between 1965 and 1980. This group came to work during down economic times. Such words as *independent, self-efficient, flexible, resourceful,* and *willing to take risks* have been used to describe them. They are the best-educated group of people ever, and they are far more adept at using technology than their predecessors. Within the United States, workers from this group are more ethnically diverse than workers in previous generations. Unlike older workers, they are not as concerned about who they work for, making them less loyal to any one company. This group is most comfortable with technology generated training.

- Generation Y—born in the 1980s and 1990s and also called the millennials or Net generation. These are the people who are most at home with technology, having literally grown up with rapidly developing new electronic marvels, and they are capable of using more than one electronic tool at a time. They are confident and motivated to achieve, and they have a lot of energy. They want feedback in order to determine how well they are performing. They're also team focused and prefer meaningful work, including work that doesn't harm the environment. This group is ready to train anywhere, anytime, using any and all technology.

It's entirely possible to find all four categories in your line-up of learners, and most likely you'll have two or more. A word of warning: describing groups of learners this way can easily lead to stereotyping, which is to be avoided completely. On the other hand, being aware of the differences among learners will help you avoid problems in the training session. Several tips for how to accommodate multiple generations were presented in Step Five, Deliver Effectively.

Guidelines for Evaluating Training (Step Seven)

We are fortunate to have excellent guidelines for evaluation, including an excellent model for evaluation provided by Donald Kirkpatrick several decades ago. Asking appropriate questions, which can be determined in advance, can contribute to effective evaluation, as well as identifying benchmarks to assist training evaluation.

Kirkpatrick's Model

The training evaluation model developed by Donald Kirkpatrick (*Evaluating Training*, 3rd ed. [Berrett-Koehler, 2006]) in the 1950s still serves as an excellent way to view how training should be evaluated. Like so much of the fundamentals of training (e.g., learning principles), a solid foundation for looking at training was built long ago. What's changed is primarily the way training is delivered. Many other successful models have been evaluated since then, and you are encouraged to research and study them as you become more involved with evaluating training. The model consists of four levels:

1. Reactions—what were learners' reactions (e.g., did they like the training, was it time well spent, will it help them when they return to work, did they learn things they hadn't anticipated?)? This is an indicator of training success. A simple questionnaire given to learners at the end of the session will let you evaluate this. With experience, you'll be able to use this information constructively. This is particularly true when you realize there's a need to make a change in the middle of a course. Learners' body language let you know how well they're doing during the training session. This isn't possible for online learning, but e-mails, text messages, and blogs can tell you a lot (i.e., stay in touch with your learners).

2. Learning—how did the training measure up (e.g., how did learners perform on tests or other assessment methods)? Evaluation built into the training course will yield this critical information— it's directly related to learning objectives. Don't wait until the end of the course to start evaluating.

3. Transfer—did learners take their newly acquired skills or knowledge and use them at work? This is where follow-on evaluation comes in (discussed in the next section). Looking at indicators related to the training (lost time due to accidents, productivity levels, and so on) is a good way to determine transfer.

4. Results—how visible were the results of training to managers and supervisors (e.g., did production increase, did customer

complaints drop off)? This is the ultimate test—has the organization improved in the desired manner because learner performance improved from the training? Note: You'll find plenty of additional background material on the model through Web and library searches.

Each of these levels builds on the others. Ultimately, all training should achieve all four levels of results to be worth the time and money spent on it.

Follow-On Evaluation

Evaluating training at the close of the last session or lesson should be done where feasible. Learning is fresh, and you can quickly determine whether learning objectives have been met. Yet, the only way you'll ever know if the skill or knowledge has been put to its intended use is to conduct evaluation after the fact—at a reasonable time after training completion (i.e., when enough time has elapsed that learners should be fully applying the skills and knowledge they acquired). This can be done by a formal method such as a questionnaire to be filled out by learner and supervisor or by a simple phone call or e-mail message. Keep the evaluation questionnaire and the method of getting it simple for the best results.

Here are some of the questions to ask for a follow-on evaluation:

Questions for the learner:

- Have you used the new skills or knowledge gained in the course?
- How soon after returning to work did you use them?
- How adequate was the training—i.e., should there have been more or less (and, if so, in which specific area)?
- Do you feel your new skill and/or knowledge is contributing to the effectiveness of your organization?
- What, if anything, should be done to improve this particular training for future learners?
- What feedback have you received from your immediate supervisor regarding training results?

Questions for the supervisor:

- What evidence have you seen that the learner was able to apply objectives achieved in the training course?
- Has the training made him or her more effective on the job?
- Why has it done so (or not done so)?
- What changes would you recommend to improve the training?
- Would you send others to receive this training (please include specifics for your answer)?

A few general tips:

- When there are large numbers of learners, such as for a company-wide training course, it may be more practical to poll a randomly selected percentage of learners for follow-on evaluation comments (possibly focusing on those who did well and those who were marginal).
- When comments from either learners or supervisors are extreme (either good or bad), make a concerted effort to contact them to find out why. This is particularly true for those whose performance didn't improve upon returning to work.
- E-mail is always available to contact learners and supervisors, so don't hesitate to make additional, informal follow-up contacts to follow learner progress. It's the only way you can keep the training content fresh—and effective.
- Technology makes training follow-up much easier, but sometimes the personal touch, showing you care, can elicit information you might not otherwise get. If there was a personal problem, if the learner and the instructor didn't get along, or if there was some other touchy situation, the learner is more likely to respond to a personal contact.
- Bear in mind that there are many variables that, together, determine how well the training accomplished its objectives (e.g., quality of material, quality of facilitator, personal life of learners, and so on). Give due consideration to all of them.

Benchmarking

Establishing benchmarks can be a useful way to go about both evaluating training and determining return on investment. Any training that is conducted must have a sound reason behind it. Some common benchmarks that can be set and subsequently used in evaluation and determining value are these:

- Skill levels are below acceptable levels.
- Rejects are above acceptable levels.
- Customer complaints are increasing.
- New systems/computers/machines are being installed and are different enough from previous ones that training is mandatory.
- Civil rights–related complaints are increasing.
- Learners require training in order to be ready to move into higher level job openings.

Sometimes the need is more obvious than at others. Need for training has been determined during the analysis phase of training (see Step Two, Focus on Performance). This becomes a carefully thought-out benchmark for the training and should be measured as precisely as possible. The benchmark is then used as the basis for evaluating and determining the value of training.

Guidelines for Determining Return on Investment (ROI) (Step Seven)

There's a fine line between training evaluation and determining return on investment (ROI). Looking at the evaluation model described, Step Four, is actually about determining ROI. If training is properly designed and delivered, a positive ROI can be assumed. However, it isn't quite that easy, because we don't live in a perfect world (e.g., we can't control the actions of learners in the learning environment, training isn't always delivered in the most effective manner, or assumptions about how learners will react to training may have been incorrect).

Implied Return on Investment

The cost benefit of some training is essentially inherent (i.e., the training must be conducted). Some examples are:

- *Training to Implement New Technologies, Systems, or Procedures.* This includes installation of new information systems, new business procedures, new equipment that must be operated by the organization's employees, and so on. The new system, equipment, or procedure will not be effectively and efficiently used if people don't know how to use them properly.
- *Training to Comply with New Rules and Laws.* When changes are made to any of the workplace laws related to civil rights (such as the Americans with Disabilities Act or the Civil Rights Act), the workforce must know what the changes or new requirements are in order to be in compliance. To fail to comply can lead to problems and fines. There are laws, regulations, and standards, ranging from international to local, that impact organizations and the workplace.
- *Training Customers to Use the Product or Service You Sold Them.* It's critical to make sure that customers are satisfied with whatever it is you provided for them, whether it is a product or a service. This is the ultimate test to ensure that the sale is complete in all senses of the word.
- *Training Suppliers to Comply with Your Requirements.* If you're installing a new procurement procedure, taking on new products and needing new supplies in order to do so, or perhaps initiating business with a new supplier, it's important that the other company be attuned to the new or existing requirements. Training its representatives to work with you will ensure smooth implementation of the project.
- *Preparing Learners to Move Up in the Organization.* Solid organizations are known for their cultures of upward mobility for employees. Even in the slowest of economic times, turnover can leave an organization with a shortage of qualified supervisors and managers. The better the company's internal communications and working relationships, the more effective the organization can be.

Here are some additional tips for these so-called implied training situations:

- Even though these situations may dictate the need for training, it's good management practice to make sure the training is conducted in the least expensive way that will achieve desired results.

- If feasible, conduct a return on investment to confirm that the training will be justified. The point here is that the need is part of the economic justification.
- Take a "devil's advocate" role and consider what will happen if the training isn't formally conducted. Will learners learn on their own (e.g., will new suppliers take the responsibility for learning your system? Will learners learn new equipment because of previous experience?)?

One last tip—any cost justification must always be directly related to the learning objectives.

General Rules for Determining ROI

One of the first rules for ROI computation is to identify all costs. Exhibit 4-7 in Step Three presents a checklist for conducting training. Most of the line items in the list are also cost items, so it serves as an excellent place to start looking at costs. Costs for training include:

- Labor to conduct needs assessment, design, development, delivery, evaluation of a training program, and administrative time spent supporting and scheduling the training course
- Labor of learners to take the training—whether in a classroom or on their own (including travel time)
- Travel expenses for learners and facilitators, including daily living and lodging expenses
- Transportation
- Facilities rental
- Training documents (e.g., workbooks, texts, case studies)
- Off-the-shelf training materials purchased from outside vendors
- Supplies (disposable materials such as paper and pens)
- Equipment purchase and/or rental—including computer and communication systems

Cost computation is the easy part of determining ROI. The toughest is to determine the value generated by the training. Some of the factors that could be assessed are:

- *Productivity.* Did the productivity of the learners increase when they returned to the job? Are service requests handled in a more timely manner than before the training? Did the shift from old systems or equipment go smoothly?
- *Improvements in Areas Needing Attention.* Was there a reduction in customer complaints, more efficient supply of materials on a production line, or changes in other areas where training was supposed to address a need for improvement?
- Reduced waste
- Quality improvement
- Reduction in time lost to injuries
- Reduction in system and equipment downtime
- Increased employee promotions
- Improved employee relations (measured by surveys)
- Reduced employee turnover (recognizing the high cost of hiring and training new employees)
- Fewer workers compensation claims
- Happier customers (measured by surveys, as well as sales figures)

Calculating ROI on Major Training Applications

Exhibit 1-1 in Step One, Facilitate Learning, lists ten major training categories. Here are some factors that could be considered in determining ROI in each category:

- *Executive Development.* This is soft training, involving interpersonal and high-level thinking skills, and thus is much more difficult to measure. One effective way to measure such training effectiveness is through observation (e.g., was the person promoted?). The learner is being groomed for the highest level of management. Often such training is delivered as graduate-level courses, so completion of course material, in a classroom or online, is indication enough that the return justifies the expenditure. Also, knowledge of how previous learners have progressed within the organization after completing executive development courses can help determine whether the cost is justified.
- *Management Development.* This is also soft training, and the same concepts for executive development apply. However, this type of training can include practical topics, such as how to develop plans or compute return on investment of planned new products

and services, which can be measured to determine if the person achieved the desired objectives. Practical exercises to be implemented by the organization, as opposed to hypothetical exercises, can be designed.

- *Supervisory Development.* Similar to the types of training just described, these courses cover interpersonal communication and thinking skills training. Again, observation—did the newly trained supervisor handle tough personnel situations properly, for example—is a good way to determine whether the training paid off. Interviewing managers of supervisors, using structured, precise instruments, is another way to measure effectiveness of training.

- *Professional Development.* Topics within this broad category of training are easier to measure for value. If an engineer has learned how to use a new computer program to accomplish his tasks more effectively, then the return is obvious (assuming the program was predetermined to improve work effectiveness). Stress management can be measured by observing sick leave and medical costs for learners who have completed the training, or determine if their productivity improved (i.e., that their stress was reduced, making them more productive).

- *Technical Skills.* These are more straightforward and easier to measure for value. If a new procurement system designed to reduce procurement costs has been implemented, the fact that a learner successfully learns how to use the system is a sign of value added.

- *Literacy Skills.* It is assumed that this training is implemented because members of the workforce need it. If this is the case, then training cost is justified if learners can read, write, or compute more effectively after training than before it. It is further assumed that the learner needed to be able to read, write, or compute in order to be able to complete required job tasks. Review the skills required for information literacy (Step One, Facilitate Learning), and you'll see that almost everyone can continue to improve in this vital skill.

- *Marketing and Sales.* Sales training can be justified because sales staff must be familiar with new products and services in order to sell them to customers. For motivational training, increase in sales is the measure of return on investment.

- *Safety and Health.* Safety training is cost justified on the basis of the level of risk present when safe practices are not observed. There are often government laws and regulations that require such training, and a fine—or a serious accident—may be the alternative to not conducting training. Health training is becoming more cost-effective because of the ever-increasing costs of employee health benefits. Reduction in claims—and organizational costs—is an excellent measure of return on investment in this area of training.
- *Orientation.* The purpose of this training is to get new employees into a productive mode as quickly as possible. The level and detail of orientation should be just that which accomplishes this objective. Measurement is therefore based on new employees' contribution to achieving organizational objectives. Note: It's relatively easy to determine if there isn't enough orientation, because the new learner may have difficulty becoming productive within the new work environment if training was inadequate.
- *Organization Development.* Organization-development interventions to make proactive organizational change may often be done through training programs, either as the intervention itself or as part of a larger set of interventions. If the intent is to make the organization more customer-friendly, for example, then training results can be measured by reduction in customer complaints. Improvement in quality is the measure of return on a quality-related organizational intervention. Return on investment for culturally focused change interventions, however, isn't as easy to measure. Return may not be measured until such time as all cultural change efforts have been completed.

For all these, every effort must be taken to ensure that whatever delivery method is selected will be the one that costs the least—and gets the job done.

Here's a fundamental rule to follow: The more thorough the front-end needs assessment and definition of learning objectives, the better able you'll be to conduct an evaluation and assess return on investment.

Professional Development Guidelines
(Step Seven)

The field of training and development has long been supported and nurtured by the American Society for Training and Development (ASTD).

ASTD's Competency Model

ASTD comes to mind when professional development is discussed. And for good reason. The organization over the years has made great strides in developing guidelines for the training and development industry. The result is the ASTD Competency Model. Details of the program are available online and from either ASTD headquarters or a local chapter. However, here's a brief overview to give you an idea of how intricate and important a formalized professional development program can be. There are many other fine training-related organizations, but this discussion concentrates on ASTD.

The model consists of roles and areas of expertise and functional competencies. The components of each of these provide an excellent overview of skills trainers need to acquire and use.

The roles are:

- Learning strategist
- Business partner
- Project manager
- Professional specialist

There are nine areas of expertise:

- Career planning/talent management
- Coaching
- Delivering training
- Designing training
- Facilitating change
- Improving performance
- Managing learning
- Managing knowledge
- Measuring/evaluating

The competencies are categorized into three groups:

- Interpersonal
- Business/management
- Personal

The model confirms the skills and functions of the trainer, as noted throughout *The First-Time Trainer, 2nd Edition*. It covers a wide range of competencies, making it clear that trainers, no matter how experienced, must continually update their skills. As they are busy adding to and improving learner skills, trainers are equally busy maintaining their own. When you investigate the topics covered in not only ASTD's training materials but in those of other suppliers as well, you will further confirm the skills you will need to acquire and keep honed to be put to best use.

Some General Guidelines to Follow

Professional development can be done in many ways—the method you choose should be the one that best fits your needs, time, and resources. Here are some general points to consider as you choose the best way to improve your skills:

- *Timeliness.* Don't engage in learning, say, a new e-learning software program, unless you'll be using it soon after completion. Judge for yourself how long you can retain newly learned skills without exercising them. A corollary to this, however, is: When in doubt, go ahead and learn the new skill—opportunities to do so may be difficult to come by in the future.
- *Targets of Opportunity.* Despite the preceding point, don't let an opportunity pass by to acquire a new skill. For example, if you're working for a temporary placement agency and they offer a course you might use, take advantage of it. Then be sure to do everything possible to use the new skill. If you have the chance to sit in on a demonstration of a new product offered by a training vendor, take advantage of it.
- *Immediate Use.* The cliché "it goes without saying" applies here. Use newly gained skills as soon as you can, and work hard at increasing your level of competency—and move toward mastery (see Step Three, Focus on Learning). This is what turns good

trainers into great ones. Look for ways you can implement new skills, even if as a volunteer.

- *Your Learning Style.* Determine how you learn best and use that method to the greatest extent possible. If you do well reading, then seek out all the written material you can. If you do well surfing the Web and interacting with online programs, then search and find useful topics for your trainer portfolio (see Resources). It wouldn't hurt if you spent time developing a learning style that doesn't ordinarily suit you, particularly if it's one useful for online learning, for example. The more learning styles you can apply productively, the better off you'll be.

- *Trainer's Portfolio.* Keep this up-to-date and make it known. If others within your organization, or outside contacts if you're an independent trainer, know of your capabilities, there's a greater chance you'll get to use them. Continually try to match what you can do to whatever training activities need doing. A word of warning: Make sure everything in your portfolio is authentic— that you can produce the goods.

- *Advertise Your Portfolio.* There are many ways to do this, particularly online. (However, be always aware of the need to protect your privacy.)

- *Volunteer Anytime There Is an Opportunity to Do So.* This is an excellent way to put new skills to use, even if your own employer, or client if you are an independent trainer, doesn't need them. Refer to Step Eight, Improve Continuously, for examples of volunteering opportunities. This is also a great way to pay back the community that has supported you.

- *You Are in Charge of Your Own Fate.* There are organizations that hire and keep employees onboard for long periods of time. But these are the exceptions, and even these companies can hit hard times, merge, or change their minds when the economy impacts them negatively. This tip goes hand-in-hand with the encouragement to advertise your talents.

- *Coaching and Mentoring.* These are skills you may find yourself facilitating for learners. Get your own coach or mentor—or both. People who succeed often cite the person who helped them out along the way as having made it possible for them to become a star, so why not take advantage of this yourself? And don't forget, when you become a coach and/or mentor, you'll learn every bit as much as the person you're mentoring or coaching. You can do this as a volunteer or within the organization you work for. It's also another way to pay back the community that has nurtured you.

- *Scanning.* Keep an eye out for new Web sites, Webinars, Webcasts, podcasts, seminars, books, articles—anything and anyplace where you might pick up new skills. Ironically, junk mail in whatever form often leads you to possible opportunities. Web sites may offer you a sampling of their products, so if they are offering new products or skills you might use, try them out. When a new training topic becomes a need for your organization, you'll be ready to follow through with it, having some idea of what it entails.

- *Sponge Effect.* Keep current on anything and everything that might be applicable to your role as a trainer. This includes knowing the latest management news from the organization you work in and certainly being knowledgeable about your field. The more you know about the organization you're serving (profit or nonprofit) and how well it's doing, the more effective you'll be. Learning objectives will turn into organizational goals that will contribute to organizational success. Training objectives should be in lockstep with organizational objectives.

- *Turn the Tables.* Everything you do for learners, do for yourself. This is a matter of becoming self-centered from time to time and identifying what you need to do to keep yourself updated. Suggestions from experienced trainers (and particularly from your coach and mentor) will make the process more efficient.

- *Practice What You Preach.* Use the tools of technology to the greatest extent possible in managing, acquiring, and refreshing your ongoing skill-building program.

- *Make the Time.* Even if you're continually busy facilitating the learning of others, set aside a regular time (once a week, for example) to review your personal professional development agenda.

- *For Every New Skill, Software Package, and so on That You Learn, Give Serious Thought to How the Principles You Have Learned Fit the New Item.* You may find that much e-learning software, for example, uses similar principles, similar to word-processing programs. This follows closely the transfer of learning effect noted in Step Three, Focus on Learning.

- *Don't Forget That You'll Never Stop Being a Learner Yourself.*

Index

CPSIA information can be obtained at www.ICGtesting.com
Printed in the USA
LVOW11s1834101114

412918LV00002B/542/P